THE
SOUL
OF
WEALTH

THE
SOUL
OF
WEALTH

—— 50 ——
REFLECTIONS
ON **MONEY**
AND **MEANING**

DANIEL CROSBY

Harriman House

HARRIMAN HOUSE LTD
3 Viceroy Court
Bedford Road
Petersfield
Hampshire
GU32 3LJ
GREAT BRITAIN
Tel: +44 (0)1730 233870

Email: enquiries@harriman-house.com
Website: harriman.house

First published in 2024.
Copyright © Daniel Crosby

The right of Daniel Crosby to be identified as the Author has been asserted in accordance with the Copyright, Design and Patents Act 1988.

Paperback ISBN: 978-1-80409-103-6
Hardback ISBN: 978-1-80409-044-2
eBook ISBN: 978-1-80409-045-9

British Library Cataloguing in Publication Data
A CIP catalogue record for this book can be obtained from the British Library.

To Katrina, who completes my soul
To Charlotte, Liam, and Lola, my world

CONTENTS

INTRODUCTION

KHALED HOSSEINI, A distinguished Afghan-American novelist, goodwill ambassador, and former physician, is perhaps best renowned for *The Kite Runner*. The acclaimed novel captivated readers through powerful storytelling and poignant themes of family and friendship set against a backdrop of political unrest and Afghanistan's turbulent history.

The novel's primary narrative centers around the journey of two boys, Amir and Hassan, whose friendship is tested by betrayal. Within the larger story, Hosseini weaves in the tale of a humble man, poor by all financial measures, who is content through a loving relationship with his wife.

One day the protagonist of the story within the story comes across a magic cup and learns that if he weeps into the cup, his tears will turn into pearls. Being a man of joy, shedding tears was a rare occurrence, so he had to conjure up reasons to feel sadness in order to get rich. The man begins to manufacture sadness and as his pearl stash swells, so does his insatiable greed.

The story reaches a tragic climax, depicting the man perched atop a mountain of pearls, gripping a knife, and weeping uncontrollably into the sorcerous cup over his slain wife.

The sequence illustrates the destructive power of unchecked

avarice, revealing how a cold pursuit of wealth can lead an ordinary person to very dark places.

We have all known people like the man in the story, who sought so diligently for ever-greater wealth that they lost themselves in the process. In fact, like me, you may have been that person yourself from time to time.

Recognizing this tendency, one of history's greatest teachers cautioned his disciples against this very thing: "For what is a man profited, if he shall gain the whole world, and lose his own soul? Or what shall a man give in exchange for his soul?" (Matthew 16:26, KJV).

Humankind finds itself at a strange crossroads; we know intuitively that true wealth—real wealth, soulful wealth—is about far more than mere money. Yet, far too often, we act as though money is an end unto itself, sacrificing some of the richest parts of our lives in its pursuit.

I have authored two books aimed at helping investors understand their behavior and the behavior of financial markets, to optimize their personal financial outcomes. *The Soul of Wealth* can be viewed as a companion to *The Laws of Wealth* and *The Behavioral Investor*, and as a guide to spending, saving, investing, and giving in ways that enrich life. As we will see in the pages ahead, maximizing returns and maximizing life are complementary, mutually important aims.

I neither vilify nor exalt wealth, opting instead for lessons on how money is less an innate good or evil and more a tool that can be used for considerable blessing or ill.

The 50 short essays that follow combine historical happenings, behavioral science research, and practical application, and were purpose-written for reading, contemplation, and implementation. I hope that you find this a page-turner, but confess that you might gain greater value from savoring and discussing each brief essay with a friend, family member, co-worker, or client, rather than through binge reading.

Throughout, the concept of 'soul' is defined as "emotional or intellectual energy or intensity, especially as revealed in a work of art or an artistic performance."

Without intentional awareness, the shallow pursuit of wealth can strip wealth of its essence. However, by engaging in thoughtful introspection, experimenting with new ways of being, and pursuing soulful living, money can serve as the transformative tool it is meant to be.

It is my goal that *The Soul of Wealth* will challenge your thinking, rekindle forgotten truths, and empower you to embrace a more energized and emotionally honest relationship with your money.

We begin by looking at why soulful wealth isn't really about the numbers at all.

WEALTH ISN'T ABOUT THE NUMBERS

L ET'S FACE IT, if you're reading this book, you're likely a bit of an overachiever. Books about wealth and happiness aren't the typical fare of couch potatoes. And as a fellow neurotic... erm, overachiever, I share your fascination with setting and achieving big goals.

Imagine for a moment that you accomplish all your goals, including your 'stretch' goals. Driven person that you are, you will likely set new, bigger, and bolder ones. You might also shift around the goalposts to keep your eyes on some future prize.

But even if we achieve one success after another, you and I will still fall short of the accolades earned by Alexander the Great, the legendary king of Macedonia. By the age of 30, he had built up one of the world's largest empires. Geographically, he had power over lands stretching from Greece to northwest India. Undefeated on the battlefield, he was widely regarded as among history's greatest military thinkers.

Toward the top on Alexander's resume was his conquest of the mighty city of Tyre. A coastal city, located on an island, it was considered to be impregnable with its formidable defenses, but Alexander was determined to capture it. The siege of Tyre was crafted by Alexander in 332 BC as part of a broader campaign against the Persians. He established a blockade during the seven-month conquest, then built a causeway—truly an engineering marvel at the time—to erect siege towers with catapults atop. Ultimately, his soldiers breached Tyre's defenses. He was said to be so heated about how Tyrians defended their city, killing a sizable portion of his men, that Alexander destroyed half the city.

It was a monumental victory and sent a message to the rest of the world. For a commander like Alexander the Great, surely a feeling of pride and some chest-pounding was deserved.

That did not happen.

Alexander felt profound disappointment and heartache. During the siege of Tyre, he lost one of his most crucial generals, who was also his closest friend. Hephaestion died from illness, and it devastated Alexander emotionally. It's said that their friendship was among the most enduring in history.

Grieving deeply, Alexander could hardly consider the victory at Tyre a sweet win. Some accounts portray him as so grief-stricken and emotionally unstable following Hephaestion's passing that the once calculating and strategic Alexander turned reckless. He was known to drink heavily afterward, potentially a contributing factor to his death at age 32.

While the loss of his confidant may not have directly led to Alexander's downfall, there's little doubt that the event played a pivotal role and even prompted him to make off-center decisions. His health and well-being were in bad shape as a result of refusing to eat or drink, while he reportedly had the physician who failed to save Hephaestion executed. Alexander's military prowess also diminished in his later years as he became preoccupied with seeing himself as divine, more than just a powerful man.

Was losing a dear friend the root of Alexander's demise? That might be a stretch. There were many factors at play—one thing in life often impacts another, and a new sequence of challenges ensues. It's clear, however, that Hephaestion's death was a turning point for both Alexander and the empire he ruled over.

For 15 years, the king never met defeat. His wartime triumphs made him the second wealthiest person of all time, surpassed only by Genghis Khan. Estimates of his net worth vary widely (there weren't exactly zeroes in a checking account in 325 BC), ranging between $1.6 trillion and $32 trillion. But whatever the actual number, Alexander was rich in a way that is nearly incomprehensible to the modern mind. By the most conservative estimate of his wealth, he was ten times richer than Jeff Bezos. By that same low estimate, he surpasses the collective wealth of the ten richest individuals globally today; people who fly to space for kicks and have private islands.

And yet, with all his opulence, all his power, he was undone in large part by something so very human—the death of someone he cared about. Alexander's sad story tells us something very real about true wealth; we tend to chase a number as an external marker of riches, but real, soulful wealth is about much more than a number.

―――――

A tragic illustration of society's tendency to pursue numbers at the expense of values is seen in how we establish and tailgate goals as we journey through life, compared to when we reflect upon our years. For those in their prime, goals generally center around a number of predictable categories like fitness and money. According to a Gallup survey conducted in late 2022, seven in ten Americans planned to set some kind of New Year's resolution.[1] For goal-setters in 2023, the top three categories were fitness (80%), financial goals (69%), and then career goals (59% for those of working age).

If you're anything like me, these goals may feel quite familiar and align with the ones we set (and probably forget) around the beginning of each new year.

For those in reflection at the end of life, though, the perspective on goals takes a profound shift. A 2012 study on the regrets of the dying highlighted five sentiments:[2]

1. They wished they had not worked so hard.
2. They regretted living a life that was not true to themselves.
3. They felt remorse for not having had the courage to express their feelings.
4. They wished they had stayed in closer touch with friends.
5. They lamented not having let themselves be happier.

What do you notice?

None of the things, not one, that seem to matter so much to us as we move through life make the list of what's important when the imminence of death has brought what truly matters into such sharp relief. Work, one of our primary aims in times of health, emerges as one of our most significant regrets when we reminisce on life.

I posed this disconnect to Twitter (now X) and received poignant replies. "The short-term list is more about 'measures,' while the long-term list is more about 'meaning'," said one individual. A financial planner remarked, "We are confused creatures who don't see the truth until there is no time left."

Those were great observations, and the same dynamic extends to how we view retirement. For most people, retirement is their single biggest financial goal. And why not—it's a distant and somewhat ambiguous milestone that will most assuredly require vast sums of wealth to achieve. Investors tend to simply chase a bigger number on a spreadsheet, constantly shifting around those goalposts mentioned earlier, and we all too commonly fail to prepare for the other, non-financial facets of retirement. Retirement is also appealing since we also generally don't like work. The nine-to-five drudgery is seen as robbing us of freedom, and enduring multiple Zoom meetings each day hardly sparks joy.

But, for all its annoyances, work still serves as a source of engagement and socialization for most people, which has a positive impact on our happiness. Consider Martin Seligman's PERMA framework—a scientific model for human flourishing—and how many of the boxes on said model are checked by work:[3]

- **Positive emotion**: Hedonic pleasure; what we think of when we think of 'fun'. Think reading a good book, going on vacation, or eating ice cream with a loved one.
- **Engagement**: Deploying skills, talents, and experience in service of an immersive task. At its best, this is what work is.
- **Relationships**: Support from, socialization with, and connection to others. For many, work is a primary source of relational connection. Some retirees quickly realize that they depended on those relationships during their careers.
- **Meaning**: Working in service of something bigger than self, including religion, spirituality, political action, activism, family, community, and yes, even work itself.
- **Accomplishment**: Being demonstrably better today than you were yesterday. The idea of accomplishment is implicit in work and is actively measured and recognized, but much less so in traditional retirement settings.

We commit so much effort trying to get to a financial number for retirement, yet we often overlook other elements of life that bring joy. Is it any wonder then that retirees are far more depressed than both the population broadly and same-aged non-retirees in particular?

My ask of you is to revisit the PERMA model, find one of the five categories where you may currently be deficient, and commit to one small action that will move you in the direction of greater fulfillment in that pillar. It should take no more than ten minutes per day initially, but will hopefully blossom into a habit that can prepare you for happiness, just as surely as you are preparing for your retirement by saving money.

Alexander devoted his short life to the conquest of nations and hoarding treasures, eventually becoming the second richest person in history, only to have his achievements unravel at the loss of a cherished relationship. Similarly, we labor for decades to reach a certain financial milestone, only to fall into a deep malaise when we realize that other paths to flourishing have been neglected. We spend our lives setting goals focused on career advancement and amassing wealth that, when the clarity of life's brevity is before us, seems like wasted time.

True wealth is not about finish lines or numbers; it's about using whatever material abundance we have to enrich the other, more enduring, paths to fulfillment. Money can buy us simple pleasures like ice cream (Positive emotion), cherished memories on vacation with people we love (Relationships), and freedom to engage in spiritual and political pursuits (Meaning), all of which can bolster our joy in real ways.

However, if we relentlessly chase wealth as an end unto itself at the expense of other facets of well-being, history and science both teach us that it will lead to a hollowing out of life and an impoverishment of spirit.

GIVING IS
THE PATH TO
ABUNDANCE

T HE WORLD APPEARS to be highly fragmented from a philosophical perspective. There are hundreds of varieties of belief and non-belief, and not one of them sums anywhere close to claiming a majority of the global population as adherents. In a very real sense, whatever you believe or don't believe, most other people disagree with you!

But if we delve beyond this superficial and cynical perspective, we uncover a surprising amount of common ground rather than disagreement in our shared worldviews.

Ideas like compassion, kindness, justice, integrity, and nonviolence are shared by most cultures and creeds, although their expressions of these tenets come from different philosophical and scriptural texts. And one such cross-cultural truism is the paradox that giving is the path to greater abundance.

The Bible tells us in Proverbs 11:24–25 that, "One person gives freely, yet gains even more; another withholds unduly, but comes to poverty. A generous person will prosper; whoever refreshes others will be refreshed."

The Tao Te Ching, an ancient Chinese text, advises, "The wise man does not lay up his own treasures. The more he gives to others, the more he has for his own."

The Hindu scripture, the Bhagavad Gita, teaches us that, "A gift is pure when it is given from the heart to the right person at the right time and at the right place, and when we expect nothing in return."

Rumi, the Sufi poet, believed that "Givers are like the ocean; they never empty, because they are always being filled from within."

Voices from every spiritual heritage across millennia and around the world have all espoused the same idea: Generosity is a paradoxical path to greater abundance.

But what does the academic research say?

Numerous studies have shed light on the significant impact of giving on the well-being of the giver, often surpassing the benefits experienced by the recipient.

In a notable paper titled "Spending Money on Others Promotes Happiness," the authors found that the way individuals choose to spend their money is as crucial as the amount they earn in determining their level of contentment.[4]

The findings go on to suggest that prosocial spending is associated with increased happiness levels, irrespective of the participants' income. Furthermore, when the 632 subjects of the study unexpectedly received a cash windfall, their happiness levels increased significantly not when splurging on themselves, but when they spent the money for the benefit of other people, even controlling for their pre-windfall happiness levels.

So, next time you receive a tidy bonus at work, maybe try doling some of it out to friends, family, or even strangers.

Arguably the most widely known part of this research involves an experiment where participants were given either $5 or $20 with the instruction to spend it by the end of the day. Those directed to use the modest amount on others or to make charitable donations reported higher post-windfall happiness than individuals told to indulge for themselves. Being generous and helping our fellow human is the more abundant path, so the evidence suggests.

The question is, why doesn't spending money on ourselves bring long-lasting joy? It's to do with the hedonic treadmill—our happiness levels tend to adjust to our circumstances over time. Those shiny new things we buy might give us a temporary thrill, but the excitement quickly wears off. When we improve the lives of others, though, a deeper enrichment endures.

The authors of the "Spending Money on Others" study went on to identify a key gap. Despite the clear advantages of generosity, the research revealed that people tend to allocate a significantly larger chunk of their income toward their personal spending priorities rather than on prosocial endeavors—we're talking a 10:1 ratio here.

But there's hope for us all. The findings show that even a minor change, like handing a $5 bill to someone in need, holds the power to produce nontrivial gains in happiness on a given day. This discovery highlights the transformative ability of small acts of kindness and demonstrates that anyone can make a positive impact, regardless of their circumstances.

However, there is another critical gap that requires attention. In a different part of the study, participants were presented with a choice between personal and altruistic spending to maximize their own gratification, and a majority (69 out of 109) thought that personal spending would make them happier than being generous. Although the research plainly shows that altruism brings more happiness than personal spending, the notion that giving is the path to abundance has yet to go mainstream.

Another set of research in 2017 aimed to investigate the actual neural mechanisms underlying the link between generosity and happiness. Subjects in an experimental group committed to spending a weekly endowment on others, while a control group agreed to spend on themselves. Using FMRI data, it was observed that the group of individuals who engaged in giving reported heightened levels of happiness. Moreover, brain scan data indicated a surge of activity in reward-related regions associated with happiness. The findings suggest that such changes in the brain promote a positive feedback loop, thereby encouraging individuals to take part in further acts of generosity.[5]

Thus, there is something in our brain that craves giving and rewards actions that stimulate it. During the worst of the Covid-19 pandemic, giving rose 6% as the crisis unfolded, a trend that surprised some researchers.[6] It begs the question: Was our innate desire to give an emotional response to the collective need for upliftment during those trying times? At the very least, it's a conjecture that might help restore your faith in humanity.

Further reinforcing this idea is a 2013 study that analyzed data from 136 countries. The conclusion was that people worldwide experienced emotional benefits when they used financial resources to support others. The tendency persisted across economic conditions, even in the absence of social ties. The findings strongly indicate that the emotional rewards derived from helping other individuals are deeply ingrained in human nature, transcending cultural and economic boundaries.[7]

What's more, the thesis that giving leads to abundance holds true regardless of age. A research paper from 2012 titled "Giving Leads to Happiness in Young Children" elucidated the concept of a 'warm glow' individuals felt after acts of kindness. Surprisingly, this feeling was most pronounced among children. Even toddlers as young as two years old derived greater happiness from giving treats to playmates rather than receiving treats themselves. Additionally, children experienced increased happiness when engaging in costly giving, willingly sacrificing their own resources, compared to giving without personal cost.[8] I suspect I speak for most parents when I say that some of my proudest parenting moments have come as I've observed my own children act selflessly, and then watched them reap the joyful benefits of that giving.

———————

OK, so being charitable makes us happy, from a young age and across cultures, but does it actually make us richer, as some researchers contend?

In some ways, that doesn't make much sense—after all, shouldn't giving away a portion of your resources diminish your own wealth? That may be the case in the most literal sense, but there still seems to be some magic around generosity. According to Ken Honda, author of the influential 2014 book *Happy Money*, those who give to charity often feel wealthier than those who do not, regardless of their income level.[9]

Surely you want to get on the path to abundance, right? Here's how you can feel that warm glow that results from happier spending:

- **Start small**: One impediment to giving is that we think it has to be a grand thing. But just take a baby step, and note the impact on aspects of your life, such as your budget and personal happiness. Just one small move toward giving is often enough to make a difference and reshape how you view your financial resources.
- **Give of yourself**: Remember, giving doesn't solely revolve around money. You can also contribute your time and talents, allowing you to see impacts firsthand. Giving of yourself is personally gratifying and can be accomplished within any budget.
- **Make it meaningful**: Reflect on what holds significance to you. For instance, my biggest charitable contribution of each of the past five years has been a gift to the psychology department of my alma mater to help young psychologists further their training. Although I trained as a clinician, I've spent my professional life studying the intersection of money, mind, and meaning. I have

had an incredible career and have hopefully helped some people along the way, but I also mourn the lives I could have touched had I chosen to remain a practicing psychologist. Helping other psychologists do the work I didn't do is a way to give back that is personally meaningful to me and my life. What would *your* meaningful giving look like?

- **Diversify**: This may be a money nerd thing, but I have lately gotten into the habit of diversifying my giving portfolio in the same way I would think about diversifying a basket of investments. Here's what I mean: A portion of our family giving goes to what philanthropy experts refer to as "effective altruism," which is charitable gifts with an extreme bang for the buck in terms of saving lives. Think mosquito nets in developing countries—inexpensive, but with enormous life-saving power. Another of our giving buckets is for things that make life worth living and are personally meaningful to us: Mental health efforts for me, and gifts to the arts for my wife, a talented visual artist and pianist. Consider how you can optimize a diversified portfolio of giving that encompasses personal effort, effective altruism, and causes that hold deep meaning to you.

Scriptures and empirical evidence converge on a common truth about money and happiness: Giving is the best path to having true abundance. We truly enrich the world and our own lives when we are generous with others.

MONEY IS A TOOL, BUT NO TOOL FIXES EVERYTHING

ENGINEERING AND TECHNOLOGY can produce world-changing innovations. The right tools in capable hands allow businesses to run more efficiently, make our everyday lives easier, and, as we've seen in the financial industry, can bring down the cost of investing. Bad tools can lead to mediocre, if not dangerous, products and outcomes, however. Toss in some haphazard construction processes, and you have a recipe for disaster.

That is precisely what happened in the Great Molasses Flood of 1919.[10]

In January of that year, a giant tank of sticky stuff burst open in Boston's North End, releasing more than two million gallons of molasses onto busy streets. Picture a massive molasses wave, moving at 35 miles per hour, dousing everything that stood in its path. Ultimately, 21 lives were lost and more than 150 people were injured. Residents could smell the spill's residue for decades after the catastrophe. The sudden event was not without cause—a confluence of factors, including poor tools and poor construction, led to the disaster.

This makes for the perfect History Channel documentary on a rainy afternoon. As the story goes, engineering and managerial mess-ups were plentiful. First, the steel tank holding the molasses was shoddy: Nearly a century later, a 2014 analysis found that a flawed rivet design made the tank's walls, which were already too thin, vulnerable to structural failure. Also, the steel used in the building's construction had been mixed with too little manganese, which made the structure brittle in frigid conditions. Then, as temperatures rose in the daytime, the molasses expanded, pressuring the weak walls and its poorly executed riveting. Fatal weak points emerged.

Problems began even before the tank was first filled, as well. Engineers knew better at the time of construction, but there was pressure to craft the 2.5-million-gallon tank quickly to meet the rising demand for industrial alcohol during World War I. The tank's overall design was defective as it had a flat shape and shallow profile, putting added strain on the walls.

Before the spill, there were signs of potential trouble. Groaning sounds were heard as the tank was being filled, and cracks developed in the days leading up to the January rupture. It was even common for children to fill cups from the emerging cracks. Regular inspections and adherence to proper safety protocols would have likely identified such obvious red flags. Alas, the 58-foot-high tank burst on that fateful mild January day, sending molasses onto the roadways and adjacent sideways, pinning victims to the ground. Experts say that had the event occurred on a hot July afternoon, the substance would have been able to spread out even further from the tank, causing even more devastation.

The right design, higher-quality materials, the proper safety measures, and paying attention to warning signs may have averted the Boston Molasses tragedy. The incident serves as a stark reminder that a practical idea must be complemented by competent individuals at the helm, along with the right tools for the project.

The deadly calamity proves that no tool is fit for every purpose; just as a hammer is useless when painting a room.

The same concept applies to our money.

Wealth can no doubt make life easier by allowing us to shed unwanted tasks and use our time more freely. Issues arise, however, when we act as if money will solve every challenge we encounter.

Let's look at some problems that money does and does not solve. As we analyze these areas, I would like for you to candidly reflect on how you use money in your own life.

Here are some problems that money can help to solve:

- **Buying time**: Time is precious, and money offers us the opportunity to spend more of it on loved ones, taking part in activities we enjoy, and freeing ourselves from unpleasant or time-consuming work. So, buying time is one of the highest and best uses of money.
- **Providing novelty**: Sometimes we just need a break from mundane life. Few activities are more stimulating than exploring a new city, trying the culinary delights of another culture, and becoming ensconced in different customs. Ergo, the novelty of travel is shown to be a worthwhile use of money in order to take our happiness up a notch. Research from Cornell University found that spending on new and exciting experiences rather than on material goods leads to more enjoyment for your buck.[11]
- **Investing in self**: Self-improvement is a valuable aspect of personal growth, but it can be pricey. Having enough money empowers us to invest in healthy food, massages, personal trainers, therapy, and other forms of self-care, all of which prevent problems later in life. Compounding returns are seen

when you invest in your health, as well as when you invest your money.

- **Education and skill development**: Learning is a powerful activity to enrich our lives. It opens new vocational doors and increases our earnings potential. Pursuing higher education and skill development, if you have the financial means, can lead to improved job prospects and overall life satisfaction. And, by the way, a college degree is still worth it. According to a report from the Georgetown University Center on Education and the Workforce, college grads today are on track to earn a median of $2.8 million over their careers, compared to $1.6 million for those who only have a high school diploma.[12] Owning an undergraduate degree also betters your chances of marrying and reduces the likelihood of divorce. There are health benefits, too: College graduates have lower rates of type 2 diabetes and heart disease, in addition to living longer than their non-college-grad peers.[13]
- **Healthcare**: Enough money can afford the best healthcare. Estimates vary, but you should expect to dole out at least $400,000 for health-related expenses in your lifetime (in today's dollars).[14] And then there is the famous Fidelity Investments study that says the average retired couple age 65 in 2023 may need upwards of $315,000 to cover healthcare expenses.[15] Wouldn't it be nice not to sweat about paying all those medical bills?

Wealth has the power to improve lives and even cure some ills, but it is not a panacea. Here are some problems that money cannot address:

- **Happiness**: You probably figured this one out already, but let's use one of our lifelines here. Phone psychologist Martin Seligman, and we'll hear that money can help with certain facets of gaining and maintaining happiness, but cash falls short of delivering true happiness. His PERMA model is a highly regarded theory of well-being and positive psychology. It posits that critical aspects of well-being are deeply influenced by our internal experiences, relationships, and a sense of purpose—all of which are very little helped by money. The relationship between money and happiness is complex and interwoven, but it is far from one-for-one. If you think that more money automatically means more happiness (and most people do), you're wrong.

- **Relationships**: Seligman's PERMA model also dives into how positive relationships are vital to rich, lasting happiness. If you could only have one thing to improve your life, strong relationships would be it, but money's tie to relationships is nuanced. Ample financial resources can afford you a trip with your family, but they can also complicate and fracture existing relationships. And cash cannot replace the emotional depth of fellowship.

- **Meaning and purpose**: As Maslow's hierarchy suggests, only after our basic needs are met can we focus on higher needs such as meaning and self-actualization. To paraphrase Gandhi, to the hungry, God can only appear as bread. In that light, money may help free us to *think about* purpose, but it cannot do the hard work of *giving* us purpose.

The belief that money is a tool that solves every problem is so hard to shake because it is riddled with half-truths:

- Money can't buy us happiness outright, but it can buy us the absence of misery.
- Money can't buy us love, but it can buy us chocolate and roses.
- Money can't buy us purpose, but it can buy us time to reflect on the meaning of life.

There is no denying the positive impact that money can have, but relying on these partial truths can lead to the misconception that money is a solution for all things. This misguided belief commonly results in misallocated time and energy as we chase after material possessions that can never fully sate us.

———————————

To apply this understanding, take a moment to reflect on whether you have been relying on money as your primary tool to seek fulfillment in one of the following areas: happiness, relationships, or purpose.

Now, consider a non-financial approach that you can try this week that might be a more direct path to getting what you want.

If it's happiness, delve into your soul to suss out what experiences would stimulate your senses. Start small by taking a different route to work, then think big about where to travel on your next vacation.

If it's relationships, reflect on who has shaped your life and how their efforts have perhaps gone too unappreciated on your end. A quick coffee invite with an old friend can be rewarding for both you and your pal. Or maybe you are due for a special date with your significant other.

If it's meaning and purpose, carving out time first thing in the morning for prayer, meditation, or simple quiet reflection can help you uncover that one thing you're lacking right now.

Using the wrong tools and taking shortcuts can lead to very real sticky situations in life and with your money. Use wealth for what it's scientifically shown to help with most, but deeper problems require you to strap on a different toolbelt.

COMPARISON
IS THE THIEF
OF JOY

V INCENT VAN GOGH was a man of undeniable artistic brilliance,
there's no questioning that. The world today reveres the Dutch
painter and holds him in the highest of creative esteem.

But the 19th-century artist was a complex soul, and one theory
posits that jealousy drove him, at age 35, to cut off the lower
half of his left ear with a razor blade. It's believed that he then
carefully bandaged the wound, wrapped the severed ear in paper,
and delivered it to a brothel in the French town of Arles. That's
where he had been working with fellow artist Paul Gauguin. Van
Gogh then offered the ear to a woman, instructing her to "keep the
object carefully."

The next morning, a police officer found an unconscious Van
Gogh and rushed him to a nearby hospital, where the remnants of
his severed ear were also later taken. Felix Ray, a young doctor, felt
too much time had passed to reattach the appendage. Van Gogh's
disfigured visage is immortalized in two paintings: *Self-Portrait
with Bandaged Ear* and *Self-Portrait with Bandaged Ear and Pipe.*[16]

Despite the story's constant retelling over the past century, significant aspects remain shrouded in mystery. Was it part of his ear or the whole ear that was lopped off? We're not sure. Did he leave the ear with a prostitute, a maid, or the brothel's night manager? Accounts vary.

Most critically, there is still considerable confusion about why he, you know, chopped his ear off in the first place. A 1981 paper by W. M. Runyan set forth a whopping 13 possible reasons—everything from seeking attention from a local family to re-enacting Simon Peter's act of severing the ear of a man who came to arrest Jesus before his crucifixion.[17] The common thread running through the two most widely accepted explanations has its roots in jealousy and comparison.

The long-time prevailing notion was that Van Gogh cut off his ear as an act of retaliation against Gauguin, whom he greatly admired, sometimes collaborated with, and often felt jealous of. Throughout his life, Van Gogh grappled with episodes of inadequacy and self-doubt,[18] which may have been intensified by his constant comparisons to fellow artists of the era.

Impressionism was gaining popularity during that time, and artists such as Monet and Renoir were in the limelight for their works. Van Gogh was believed to feel that his work fell short of his peers. The extensive collection of over 600 letters from Vincent to his brother, Theo, chronicles his battles with depression and self-doubt. Tragically, Vincent took his own life at the age of 37, and just six months later, Theo passed away as well.[19]

There's little doubt that Gauguin and Van Gogh fought on the day he maimed himself, and for many years it was assumed that this altercation was the proximal cause of the infamous ear incident. However, new research suggests that it may not have been jealousy toward another artist that led to this act of self-sabotage, but rather Van Gogh's insecurities concerning someone even closer to him—his brother, Theo.

One theory proposes that Vincent's decision to chop off part of his ear was inspired by news of Theo's marriage. Theo was not only his brother's confidant, but also his financier. Is it therefore possible that Theo's new life as a married man posed a threat to the intimate bond between the two brothers?[20]

It is scary to contemplate that comparison and jealousy have a place within the human heart, and that there is a real possibility they can destroy our lives, including our finances.

Just like Vincent, experimental research indicates that social comparisons around money make us sad and that looking 'up' with jealousy makes us more upset than looking 'down' with pride makes us happy.[21] This phenomenon aligns with the concept of loss aversion. In a sense, the emotional distress of a wealth gap, when we compare ourselves to richer people, surpasses the perceived satisfaction gained from having an economic edge over individuals who are less well-off than us.

According to a study performed in 2021, social comparison plays a crucial role in mediating the impact of absolute income on happiness.[22] The research found that people with mid-range salaries were happier than those with very high or very low incomes because they were able to make social comparisons in both directions as opposed to making large comparisons either up or down. The author concluded that as inequality increased within income groups, unhappiness due to social comparisons also increased.

Individuals in the middle class basically say, "Yes, some are doing better than me, but just as many are doing worse, and I feel a sense of contentment." On the other hand, individuals on the extreme ends of the income spectrum either perceive a world stacked against them, or feel that their financial aspirations are unattainable, resulting in sweeping comparisons that erode contentment.

Broader research also asserts that how we see ourselves

measuring up to others—not our absolute level of prosperity—drives our happiness or discontent. A meta-analysis published in *Psychological Bulletin* explored the relationship between wealth inequality, social comparison, and happiness. The research, which collected data on more than 2.3 million participants globally, revealed that people's subjective socioeconomic status, which reflects their perception of income, education, and occupation relative to others, is more strongly associated with happiness than their objective socioeconomic status measured by income and education levels. Densely populated countries, where competition for resources is relatively high, were seen as more likely to exhibit the effects of social comparison.

How we view ourselves relative to peers has emerged as its own branch in social psychology. Leon Festinger's Social Comparison Theory proposes that individuals have an innate drive to evaluate their abilities and attributes by comparing themselves to others.

According to Festinger's theory, people engage in social comparison to gain an understanding of their worth and to validate their beliefs and attitudes. He further suggests that social comparison serves as a means of reducing uncertainty and ambiguity in life (we hate uncertainty, as detailed elsewhere in this book). In a sense, if we were a stock, we'd look to the world to determine our fair value and whether we are on the right track.[23]

As Festinger notes, comparison is natural, but not all comparisons are created equal. Social comparison may be unavoidable, but we can be thoughtful about how and to whom we compare ourselves to avoid going mad with jealousy.

———————

Consider putting to work these strategies in your life to focus on valuing yourself for you, not based on what this jacked-up world thinks:

- **Focus on your goals and values**: Recognize that success and fulfillment look different for each individual. There's a reason my first book was titled *Personal Benchmark*. As Canadian psychologist Jordan Peterson says, "Compare yourself to who you were yesterday, not to who someone else is today."
- **Practice gratitude**: Cultivating a sense of thankfulness can help counteract any feelings of jealousy. Research has shown that practicing gratitude can increase happiness and overall well-being—one study found that people who wrote gratitude letters alongside receiving counseling reported better mental health outcomes compared to those who received counseling alone.[24]
- **Limit social media exposure**: Scientific evidence shows that excessive use of social media contributes to feelings of sadness and discontent. A 2022 meta-analysis analyzing the link between time spent on social media and depression risk revealed that the risk of depression increased by 13% for each additional hour of social media use in adolescents.[25] Consider setting boundaries on the amount of time you spend on social platforms and be mindful of how it affects your emotions. Taking breaks from social media or unfollowing accounts that trigger comparison can be beneficial for your mental well-being.
- **Be selective with your reference classes**: The ten most followed people on Instagram have an average net worth of about $400 million as of 2023, not to mention really great abs. As the studies have shown, comparing ourselves to people far outside of our financial orbit is a path to misery. Be thoughtful about your reference classes, select people who share your values, goals, and priorities, and find mentors who can provide inspiration and support on your journey.

You are not your Instagram follower count, and all those likes matter little. By homing in on an appreciation for your life and its blessings, you can avoid all the unhelpful noise in this world (and you don't have to chop your ear off either).

MEANING
AT WORK

IKE ROWE'S HIT TV show, *Dirty Jobs*, gave us the
entertaining gift of understanding the hard labor that goes
into many of the conveniences that we take for granted. From sewer
inspectors to shark suit testers to, well, cow inseminators, Rowe
showed us that our lives of ease come at a real cost to so many who
are doing important but invisible work. But of all the dirty jobs in
the world, there is only one that comes complete with a popular
phrase that speaks to the maddening nature of the work.

I'm speaking, of course, of "going postal."

The colloquial phrase describes a sudden and extreme outburst
of aggression, usually at the workplace. The term gained
prominence following a series of deadly incidents involving
postal workers in the 1980s and 1990s. These episodes of violence
on the job took place in Oregon, Oklahoma, California, New
Jersey, and Michigan. Capturing national attention, the tragic
events shed light on the intense pressure and stress faced by postal
workers, and "going postal" became part of the public discourse,
even making its way onto *Seinfeld*. Postal-employee Newman
described the frustration:

... the mail never stops! It just keeps coming and coming and coming. There's never a letup, it's relentless.[26]

Despite its reputation as being mundane, is postal work uniquely meaningless? Herodotus, Greek author of the first great narrative history produced in the ancient world, would beg to differ. The "Father of History" himself had this to say of the postal couriers who served a vital military function in the wars between the Greeks and Persians:

Neither snow nor rain nor heat nor gloom of night stays these couriers from the swift completion of their appointed rounds.

This beautiful tribute to the purpose-driven nature of postal work is etched in granite above the entrance to the New York City Post Office on 8th Avenue, if you'd like to take a look. Another inscription, less well known, can be found in the building that houses the Smithsonian Institution's National Postal Museum in Washington, D.C. It reads:

Messenger of Sympathy and Love
Servant of Parted Friends
Consoler of the Lonely
Bond of the Scattered Family
Enlarger of the Common Life

Carrier of News and Knowledge
Instrument of Trade and Industry
Promoter of Mutual Acquaintance
Of Peace and of Goodwill Among Men and Nations.[27]

So, which is it?

Are postal workers subjected to endless inanity that drives them mad, or are they the glue holding nations and families together? Often, when considering our own jobs and the work of others, we emphasize the most reductionistic, tedious, and trivial parts of our lives Monday through Friday, leading to a sense of meaninglessness. A growing body of research suggests, however, that as we begin to view our labor more holistically, we elevate it and kick off a virtuous cycle whereby work becomes meaningful, and this meaning improves the quality of the effort we put in on the job.

Postal workers interface with a sometimes-ungrateful public and perform a task that can feel rote and small. But they also deliver parcels that are true expressions of love, bring a smile to a shut-in grandparent, and link families who long for connection. Both aspects are true of postal work, and the lens through which it is viewed has a great deal to do with both how the person doing the job feels and how the work gets done.

Meaning at work is undoubtedly nice to have. What's less clear, though, is whether it positively impacts business value.

Three business professors set out to examine this very question and shared their results in their book, *Firms of Endearment: How World-Class Companies Profit from Passion and Purpose.* The authors wanted to measure the performance of "passion and purpose-driven" companies like Costco, Wegmans, Whole Foods, and IKEA, and compare them to the S&P 500 and the companies in the bestselling book, *Good to Great.*

Over the 15 years they observed these companies (1998 to 2013), the S&P 500 returned 118%, and the "good to great" firms' shares more than doubled the index's performance, returning 263% over that time. But the stocks of the "firms of endearment" companies, driven by a culture of passion and purpose, dwarfed them both with a staggering 1681% return over that period. For those playing along at home, that's a 14:1 and 6:1 return, respectively.[28]

The reasons why meaning may drive this outsized business success are undoubtedly complex, but it likely starts where most things do: with the people. According to a 2022 Harris-Kumanu Purpose Poll, 66% of those who reported high levels of purpose at work were highly engaged, compared to just 16% with middling levels of purpose and 1% with low purpose. Relatedly, 78% of those with high purpose planned to be working at the organization in two years, a figure that was less than half for those reporting just medium purpose.[29]

If meaning at work is highly predictive of engagement, productivity, performance, and share price, it's worth asking how well we are doing integrating life and labor. The numbers show that we have a lot of room for improvement. According to a 2013 poll by Gallup:

- 37% of employees clearly know the company's purpose
- 20% are enthusiastic about the purpose
- 20% see how they could support the purpose
- 15% feel enabled to work toward the purpose
- 20% fully trust the company

In another Harris-Kumanu Purpose Poll on integrating purpose with work, the largest group (50%) said that work didn't help at all, while just 17% highlighted aspects of personal growth factors such as getting out of the house, feeling successful, and staying occupied. Sixteen percent of respondents mentioned helping others and 12% cited financial reasons (keeping the lights on at home, helping their family get by, and providing money to do the things they love). Just 5% mentioned anything having to do with contributing to the team or organization—which can't make org leaders happy.

It's hard to build toward a purpose that you are not even aware of or that doesn't exist.

So, where do we go from here?

Victor Strecher's work, *Life on Purpose: How Living for What Matters Most Changes Everything*, provides a clue about what a meaningful workplace looks like. He found three common elements:

1. A sense of dignity and belonging.
2. The organization asks about and supports your purpose.
3. The organization itself has a stated purpose.[30]

It's a simple enough formula, especially when you consider the kind of results it brings about. There are likely parts of your job that are boring. After all, you go to 'work', not to 'fun'. But by learning to view those plain and often thankless aspects of your nine-to-five through a lens of meaningful maximalism instead of reductionism, you can discover your own purpose. You may not currently have your dream job, but integrating your dreams into your daily work life can deliver personal drive along with a sense of belonging (and at least you're not a sewer inspector).

YOU MIGHT BE SOLVING THE WRONG PROBLEM

T HE NIFTY FIFTY was a nickname given to the premier U.S. stocks of the 1960s and 1970s, many of which are still around. American Express, Black & Decker, Coca-Cola (a personal favorite), IBM, Pfizer, and Walmart are just a handful of the 50 that remain blue-chip stocks today.

Another household name, at least to kids of the 1980s and 1990s like me, has not enjoyed such success. Eastman Kodak dominated the photography industry decades ago. Gen X and older are familiar with what a 'Kodak moment' is, but today's youth probably has no idea what that means.

The reason?

Kodak's snapshot of the future focused on the traditional photographic film business, not the technological 180 that was to come. As stalwarts like IBM, then Microsoft, then Apple drove forward the digital and personalized-tech revolutions, Kodak failed to develop a modern business model. After dismal sales at the start of the 21st century, the embattled company shuttered in 2012. They had tried to solve the wrong problem.

Another case study in solving the wrong problem was seen in the 2000s. Blockbuster and Netflix went head-to-head during the aughts, a time when Blockbuster was best in show. The company was the premier video rental company (how antiquated does that sound today?), but its fatal flaw was a failure to adapt to changing consumer tastes. Like Kodak, emerging technology played a crucial role in its ultimate demise.

Back in, say, 2005, Netflix was merely a DVD-by-mail service firm, but co-founder and CEO Reed Hastings envisioned a streaming future. Blockbuster, meanwhile, had convinced itself that people would continue to drive to the video rental store on a Friday night to then chill at home and maybe pay a late fee after forgetting to return the tape on time, or for not being kind and rewinding.

Alas, Blockbuster's fixation on physical locations and haphazard entry into the digital space resulted in its bankruptcy in 2010. In a twist of painful irony, Blockbuster had the chance to buy out Netflix for just $50 million, but its management team laughed Netflix co-founder Marc Randolph out of the room.[31] The cost of hubris in that instance was about $200 billion (the current market cap of the streaming giant). Today, there remains a lone Blockbuster store in Bend, Oregon and—it gets better—it was the feature of a 2022 Netflix special.

Perhaps the ultimate story of solving the wrong problem was borne out by BlackBerry. To its credit, the mobile phone firm was a pioneer in its market. BlackBerry's physical keyboard was loved by businesspeople and its secure email capabilities made working on-the-go a thing before smartphones truly went mainstream in the late 2000s. That conservatism bias—the failure to timely adapt to new trends—was BlackBerry's miss. Rather than embrace consumers' affection for touch-screen technology, it dug its heels into the concept that physical keyboards would remain a primary selling point. Apple and Android ate BlackBerry's lunch. While the physical keyboard is a relic of the past, BlackBerry is still around, but it's a shadow of its former self. After peaking near $150 per share as Research In Motion in 2008, you can buy the stock today for a mere $5.

It's clear that the annals of business history are filled with stories of brilliant, blue-chip companies that solved the wrong problem. But there are also major pitfalls that can plague investors who fail to recognize the correct underlying issue.

Stress about money is maybe the granddaddy of them all. With a personal saving rate hovering around 4% and that constant compulsion to keep up with the Joneses, all too often people forgo their health in a never-ending pursuit of wealth. Consider that Americans leave about ten vacation days on the table annually, according to Qualtrics.[32] Country-wide, that sums to more than a million weeks of PTO that workers sacrifice just to try to get ahead financially. This leave from work is there for a reason—for the benefit of our physical and mental health.

It is as if we think working harder and longer will earn us that next big promotion, which will get us one step closer to money sanity. We are chasing after the wrong carrot, however. The stats are sobering. The World Health Organization found that 745,000 excess deaths take place annually due to overwork and burnout. What's more, $190 billion of annual added healthcare costs mount just from too much time on the job.[33] Solving the right problem may mean embracing time away from the office and being intentional about devoting days to being around loved ones, engaging in fun activities outside, and re-prioritizing your career within your life.

Financial TV is another area where we try to tackle the wrong problem. Market-watchers love to focus on things that are simply unknowable and out of their control. We've seen it in recent years with minute-by-minute coverage of the spread of a virus, the outcome of a war in a distant land, and the political maneuvers of presidents and prime ministers. But why do we have this obsession? Why are we drawn to wanting to know all the variables, when there is nothing we can do to influence the situation ourselves? It comes down to the *illusion of control*, in which individuals often overestimate their ability to have authority over issues.

The illusion of control, as it pertains to investment markets, commonly means always checking your account balances, flipping on CNBC, Fox Business, or Bloomberg for a few extra minutes in the morning, or constantly shifting your portfolio allocation based on near-term fear rather than long-term logic.

To solve the right problem, the first step is to admit you have little control over most external events. That dose of humility then allows your mind to make better, more rational decisions with your money.

In the end, investing isn't about beating the market; that is not the correct problem you should be trying to solve. Investing is a method to securing financial and personal freedom—however you might define that. Markets and our own portfolios are littered with percentage rates of return, which makes it so easy to compare one thing versus another and strain for the best possible rates of return.

However, for most of us normal people, determining what mix of stocks and bonds makes sense for us based on our goals and values, then going with a straightforward allocation, is wiser than aiming to beat an arbitrary benchmark or maximize returns.

We know from the annual SPIVA scorecard from S&P Global that most professional investors don't beat their chosen benchmark. Over a 20-year period, about 90% of U.S. stock mutual funds underperform their benchmark.[34] And author and behavioral finance expert Dr. Brian Portnoy found that just 5% of professionals show skill in picking the winning asset managers. So, for ordinary investors saving for retirement to try to do that is futile, and a case of trying to solve the wrong problem.

We should forget about trying to outdo a benchmark or people. As Jason Zweig frames it, "investing isn't about beating others at their game. It's about controlling yourself at your own game."[35]

———————

There are many reasons why we may be enticed to solve the wrong problem. Sometimes we are drawn in by the complexity of the problem, which makes it feel important. Other times, it is easier to worry about some externality than it is to focus on getting our own house in order. Whatever the reason, if we don't want our financial life to look like a Blockbuster store, we'd be wise to focus on solving problems that are both meaningful and within our power to influence.

THE POWER OF HABITS: THE RICHES IN REPETITION

"**T**O LOVE ANOTHER person is to see the face of God."

Victor Hugo's prose is some of the most lyrical and profound in the literary canon. Hugo is of course known for his masterworks, *Les Miserables* and *The Hunchback of Notre-Dame*, but what is perhaps less appreciated about the greatest French writer ever is that he was also an amateur behavioralist. It was Hugo's commitment to a set of disciplined habits, as much as his innate abilities, that are the reason why we are able to experience the highs and lows of humanity through his words.

Hugo had big aspirations, but he also had some tendencies that got in the way of meeting those goals if left unchecked. Like most of us, as a deadline approached, Victor would procrastinate and engage in a mix of socializing and puttering that put him at risk of missing his target date. To overcome these all-too-human tendencies, Hugo came up with a disciplined solution—it involved nudity, of all things.

As Robin Liefeld writes:

During the writing of *The Hunchback of Notre-Dame*, Hugo's routine was to lock himself in a room, often with a large wooden plank across the door to prevent anyone from entering. *He would remove all his clothes and give them to his assistant who would then be instructed to hide the clothing.*

With his clothes out of reach and nothing to wear but a large shawl, Hugo would settle down to write in solitude. This helped him to remain focused, eliminating the temptation to stop writing.[36]

The fruit of Hugo's quirky habit was volumes of work elucidating the plight of the poor and championing social justice, none of which would have been realized without his discipline.

Just as the power of habit helped Hugo bring about a series of magisterial literary works, understanding and accounting for your habits is a precursor to getting your money life in proper order.

Colloquially, we use the word 'habit' to refer to a frequent or customary action, but in psychology it has a very particular meaning that offers insights into how to shape and improve our behaviors.

For psychologists, a habit is an action that is triggered automatically in response to a contextual cue. As described by Charles Duhigg in his excellent *The Power of Habit*, the habit formation model has four stages.

1. **Cue:** The cue is a trigger that tells your brain to go into automatic mode. For example, getting into your car might be a cue for you to buckle your seat belt.
2. **Craving:** The craving is the urge to perform the habit. Sticking with the seatbelt example, the craving may be the slight unease you feel until you are securely buckled in.

3. **Response**: The response is the behavior itself. In this case, securing the belt.

4. **Reward**: The reward is the feeling of satisfaction that you get from performing the habit. The reward can be physical, such as the taste of a donut, or it can be emotional, such as the feeling of comfort that you get from not worrying about flying out of the front windshield.

Extensive psychological research over the decades shows that mere repetition of a simple action, within a consistent context, results in the activation of associative learning. That is, behaviors become habits upon certain environmental cues. Think washing hands after using the restroom.

First, in the study "Making health habitual: The psychology of 'habit-formation' and general practice," the authors mention research, including a concept called 'habit memory', which involves constant trial and error by our brains.[37] Once we mentally land upon a method to complete a task, we often stick with it, according to medical studies. Change up the setting, though, and human performance can collapse.[38]

The researchers also reference a second set of evidence suggesting that behavior through concepts such as reinforcement, motivation, and response evocation forms a chain of conditions from physical stimulus to response that is commonly repeated and persistent.[39]

Third, an experiment took 96 volunteers and tasked them to perform a daily behavior in the same setting for 12 weeks. The time it took for participants to reach 95% of their maximum automaticity varied greatly, ranging from 18 to 254 days, so it's clear that we are not all created equal in terms of habit-forming. Some methodical types might gain a consistent process quickly, while others need more reps.[40]

Repetition is shown to make people healthier, too. A 2012 study reported that simple advice can turn non-routine healthy actions into durable habits. Many healthcare professionals are hesitant to offer behavior change advice since it can be quite time-consuming to see results. But by using automatic cues, brief advice can get our repetition-loving minds to do the heavy lifting for us.[41]

If this works for MDs, why not for CFPs and CFAs? Using this method, it is no longer on us to make the psychologically difficult decision to do the right thing with our money. That tough work has now been placed upon a cue! Through the power of habit, saving and investing behavior that was once thoughtful and effortful now becomes automatic.

The beauty of habits is that they tend to endure even when conscious motivation fades away. A habit also offers respite for our minds, as the automation of common actions frees up mental resources for other tasks.[42] Since the brain accounts for roughly 20% of our body's energy use, yet is just 2% of our weight, we are constantly on the unconscious hunt to get it some rest.[43]

In the personal finance arena, so much effort is wasted trying to engender the right motivations and attitudes around money when behavior is all that matters. Attitudes change, motivation wanes, but habits are enduring. Not only do repeated actions become self-reinforcing, but as wise decisions lead to the accumulation of wealth, the rewards grow, deepening habits even further—good choices beget good financial outcomes, and round and round we go.

Revisiting the Habit Formation Model, let's create a simple framework for developing a new financial habit.

- **Step One**: Identify the habit—Suppose our hero is already maxing out her retirement accounts and wants to save just a little bit more each month, say $250, to make it measurable and specific.

- **Step Two**: Determine the cue—Our hero now needs to identify a regular cue in her life that corresponds with her goal. Nick Maggiulli, author of *Just Keep Buying*, has a rule that whenever he makes a big purchase, he must save an equivalent amount. For instance, if he were to buy a $300 pair of shoes, he would first need to save $300. Inspired by Nick, our hero decides that every time she goes out to eat, she will contribute an amount equivalent to the cost of the meal to her investment account. Thus, going out to eat becomes her cue to save.

- **Step Three**: Design the routine—The routine must be made as simple and timely as possible to maximize adherence. The protagonist streamlines the process by using a slick investing app and commits to saving before the dinner check arrives. This process ensures a simple and timely routine with built-in accountability. After all, they aren't going to let you leave the restaurant until you've paid the bill!

- **Step Four**: Create a reward—This new routine is clever because it includes baked-in rewards. Eating out treats you with delicious food, an absence of dishes in the sink, and social connectedness with friends. The positive feelings associated with saving and investing are the icing on the cake. Other habit-formation routines may be less intrinsically fulfilling, requiring regular additional rewards, such as spoken self-affirmations like, "I'm really proud of how you're looking out for your future!" or more targeted rewards at specific milestones. A combination of the two might work for you. The key is to make the behavior rewarding enough for it to become second nature.

Now, let's have some fun. According to the U.S. Bureau of Labor Statistics, the average American eats out just over five times per week, resulting in a yearly tab of $3,500.[44] Imagine if the woman in our example chose to match, save, and invest that amount, starting when she graduated from college and ending at her retirement at 65.

At the historical return rate of the S&P 500, that $3,500 would grow to a smidgen over $2 million by the time she retires.

An extreme example, but hopefully you can see the principle in action.

––––––––––

It's important to recognize that two things can be true at once: 1) It can be challenging to earn, save, and invest money if you have never started; and 2) Once started, it can become so addictive and then difficult to stop.

Whether we are talking about odd hacks for getting your book written or something more staid like financial prudence, the fact is that small behaviors, consistently applied, can develop into habits that bring about almost unimaginable growth.

THE 'WHAT' IS EASY, THE 'HOW' IS HARD

IN TODAY'S INFORMATION-DRIVEN and AI-augmented world, we have unprecedented access to vast amounts of knowledge across any topic we could possibly desire, including ways to improve our health, wealth, and happiness. Still, all of the data out there in the universe doesn't help a whole lot if we don't take action.

This is where the knowing-doing gap comes into play, a psychological term that describes the disconnect between what we know we should do and how we behave. It turns out that knowing what we ought to do and doing what we ought to have less in common than we might hope.

The *Titanic* tragedy is a classic and sorrowful example of the knowing-doing gap. There were many instances where those in charge of the ship's maiden voyage were aware of the possible perils but failed to take protective measures and corrective actions.

In the luxury liner's design, only 20 lifeboats were kept on the decks, able to hold just 1,178 people, barely more than half of the 2,240 souls on board (and well shy of the ship's 3,327 capacity). The ship's engineers and crafters were aware of this deficit. Still, they elected to only meet the bare minimum requirement. Upon colliding with the iceberg, the knowing-doing gap resulted in a shortage of lifeboats and an excess loss of life.

The crew also demonstrated this behavioral flaw. As depicted in the 1997 blockbuster film, Captain Edward Smith, among others, was cognizant of the potential dangers posed by the near-freezing North Atlantic waters. Fields of icebergs were laid out in front of the *Titanic*, yet it was full steam ahead. With warnings in hand, Captain Smith maintained the ship's heading and speed, increasing the chance of a disastrous iceberg collision.

Also seen in the movie, the crew was not trained to handle a crisis. A lack of emergency preparedness, including efficient launching and loading of the lifeboats, surely resulted in more people perishing, even considering the shortage of lifeboat capacity. The gap between knowledge and practice contributed to confusion, delays, and ineffective evacuation efforts during the chaos right before the ship foundered.

Lastly, the knowing-doing discrepancy was prevalent even before the first nail was hammered in Belfast. Overconfidence in the *Titanic's* design—it was said to be "unsinkable," after all—led to complacency in taking proper precautions. It was thought that the vessel's advanced safety features were simply good enough, so they elected to bypass steps that would have helped reduce the chance of an at-sea operational crisis.

Ultimately, those in charge knew that there were inadequate lifeboats, yet they did nothing. They knew that there were icebergs, yet they did not alter course. They knew that emergency preparedness was lacking, yet the music on the decks kept playing. With the benefit of 20/20 hindsight, it is easy for us to mock the designers of this ill-fated voyage as victims of, ahem, titanic hubris.

But to do so would ignore the ways in which all of us commonly fall victim to a huge gap between what we know we ought to do and what we actually do.

Allow me to hit you with a few examples:

- **Diet and exercise**: The *what* of maintaining a healthy weight is exceedingly simple—move more and eat less. Yet, the *how* still eludes so many of us, with 51% of the world projected to be overweight by 2035, according to a report from the World Obesity Federation.[45]
- **Smoking**: The dangers of lighting up are well documented and widely acknowledged, but more than one-third of men across the globe smoke, so says the World Health Organization.[46] More shocking still, the smoking rate among licensed practical nurses, those tasked with helping us recover from illness, is *higher* than that observed in the general population.[47]
- **Financial preparedness**: The National Institute on Retirement Security found that as of 2020, the median retirement account balance for working-age households in the U.S. is just $2,500. Additionally, the same study revealed that 62% of households aged 55–64 have retirement savings that are less than one times their annual income.[48] As well as this shortfall in retirement assets, many of us have our hands full with high-interest-rate debt. A 2023 Consumer Financial Research Bureau report forecasts Americans' total credit card balance will soon sum to a staggering $1 trillion. Spread out among 175 million card holders, and that is more than $5,700 per U.S. adult.[49] Amid the anxiety that can bring, it's frankly no surprise that 62% of Americans live paycheck to paycheck, per a 2023 survey conducted by LendingClub.[50]

And yet the *what* of money is stunningly simple. It goes something like this:

- Maximize your human capital and earnings potential.
- Set aside a meaningful percentage to save and invest monthly.

- Diversify those investments.
- Leave them alone and let time and compounding work.

That's it. That is the whole game.

And yet, we struggle, almost universally, because the *what* is easy and the *how* is hard.

It's no surprise that often the largest area in a bookstore is the self-help section. We have this arrogance inside that makes us believe that reading one more book on investing will make us as skilled at stock-picking as Warren Buffett, taking an extra course on budgeting will make us personal finance gurus, and learning about the latest diet fad will make us just three sit-ups away from looking like Brad Pitt. We think that more education around the *what* is going to do the trick.

Focusing on the *what* can feel like progress, but often it is merely a self-serving distraction from doing the grunt work of changing our behavior—that is, the *how*. Reading stories and building knowledge feels like progress, but it doesn't demand much of us. We already possess the knowledge of what needs to be done, and continuing to accumulate more information will not significantly aid progress. It's time now to shift the focus toward the more arduous task of getting started.

For those who have figured out the *what* and are looking to move to the *how*, Jeffrey Pfeffer and Robert Sutton, authors of *The Knowing-Doing Gap*, have five specific actions steps for turning knowledge into action:[51]

1. **Teach others**: Through sharing what we know, we reinforce our own understanding, cementing the knowledge in our minds. That can drive the teacher to act while also encouraging the students to do the same. Want to solidify your own learning around sound investing principles? Teach a friend or a family member.

2. **Make it tiny**: The first step in getting something done is commonly the hardest, be it an assignment at work or an item on the weekend to-do list at home. Once you begin, though, flow can build momentum. Just make the first small move. A behavior in motion tends to stay in motion, so don't be afraid to start saving 3% of your paycheck, even if your ultimate goal is 10%.

3. **Find your why**: There's more motivation when something is personal. Understanding why an action matters on an individual level helps to sustain commitment and drive. It becomes easier to say "no" to daily financial temptations if you realize that it's in service of a larger "yes." Find that "yes" and keep it front and center.

4. **Collaborate**: Engaging with like-minded and similarly driven people fosters a supportive and accountable environment. Surround yourself with people who share your goals and values, and don't be afraid to rely on and become accountable to one another.

5. **Reward the action**: Don't wait until crossing the proverbial finish line to celebrate. Offer an incentive to yourself at every minor milestone. Doing so will enhance your zeal and keep the *how* going strong.

Turns out, you do not need more knowledge, you just need to get going. And with the right people around you, purpose in your soul, and process in mind, you'll go very far indeed.

YOUR MONEY
NEEDS A 'WHY'

V IKTOR FRANKL, ALONG with Soren Kierkegaard, stands as one of my greatest professional heroes, and his book *Man's Search for Meaning* holds a place akin to personal scripture for me. There is no book that I have referenced more, and there is scarcely a day that passes that I don't consider some piece of that work.

A refrain that runs through the book is the notion that, "(S)he who has a why to live can bear with almost any how," a concept Frankl drew from Nietzsche. This idea encapsulates Frankl's philosophy of finding purpose in life as a means to endure and overcome the challenges each of us faces.

If you have not read *Man's Search for Meaning*, drop this sucker and go find a copy of Frankl's book instead.

You'll see that Frankl offers specific examples of how having a sense of purpose strengthened him to brave unimaginable conditions in his three long years at Nazi concentration camps. A poignant passage in the text describes his time at Auschwitz, where he was forced to treat fellow prisoners who were sick and wounded. While physically and emotionally difficult, Frankl found meaning in helping others. That was his motivation to persevere amidst a brutal daily reality.

With that resolve, Frankl expressed the essence of human existence:

> Being human always points, and is directed, to something, or someone, other than oneself—be it meaning to fulfill or another human being to encounter. The more one forgets himself—by giving himself to a cause to serve or another person to love—the more human he is and the more he actualizes himself.

In a more personal moment in the work, Frankl shared a touching account of a conversation he had with a fellow inmate who had seemed to lose all hope to continue. He helped the discouraged man discover his own reason to live, a purpose that provided psychological and spiritual sustenance during the torment of the camp.

Frankl's vision of life was unwavering after his release. He held a profound sense of responsibility to assist people facing anguish—whatever the situation—in finding rays of hope during their darkest moments. He later stated:

> I had wanted simply to convey to the reader by way of a concrete example that life holds a potential meaning under any conditions, even the most miserable ones. And I thought that if the point were demonstrated in a situation as extreme as that in a concentration camp, my book might gain a hearing. I therefore felt responsible for writing down what I had gone through, for I thought it might be helpful to people who are prone to despair.

Part of the value of Frankl's insights is that they were so incredibly hard-won. It's hard to imagine a set of circumstances more degrading and dehumanizing than what Frankl endured.

And yet, through it all, he was able to persevere by focusing on his 'why'. Said Frankl of this concept:

> Everyone has his own specific vocation or mission in life; everyone must carry out a concrete assignment that demands fulfillment. Therein he cannot be replaced, nor can his life be repeated. Thus, everyone's task is unique as is his specific opportunity to implement it.

While uncovering our specific calling can be arduous and winding, it's essential to embark on this journey of discovering our personal mission. What is less widely understood is that our wealth, too, should have a 'why'. We can do that by establishing the right goals based on our values.

Intuitively, aligning our money with a meaningful objective can make saving and investing more motivating, but it also turns out that a goals-based investment (GBI) strategy leads to more wealth accumulation, period.

According to research conducted in 2014 by David Blanchett, former head of retirement research at Morningstar, using a GBI framework in financial planning led to an increase in client wealth of more than 15%. What's more, individual investors found greater satisfaction when their advisors focused on their personal goals rather than arbitrary performance benchmarks.[52]

And the more human you make your goals, the better off you might be. A 2009 study by Cheema and Soman found that partitioning money into distinct buckets and pairing these buckets with visual reminders, such as a picture of the saver's family, resulted in a remarkable nearly two-fold increase in savings compared to a control group.[53]

In other research, SEI Investments found that the simple practice of renaming an investment account with something personal helps people keep their eye on the prize during periods of volatility and bear markets.[54] You have probably seen this feature if you have brokerage accounts or IRAs at some of the major investment houses. They let you rename the generic "Account 1234-5678X" as a more meaningful "Olivia's & Noah's College," or "IRA X12345678" into "Our dream house on the lake."

So, goals help with overall wealth creation, may result in higher saving rates, and they also serve as an anchor during volatility— and all you must do is give your investing account a nickname.

———————————

The benefits of tying our dollars directly to our dreams are many, but I think it boils down to two crucial aspects: roots and wings.

Wings are the motivation, the drive, the dream—our mental and emotional cornerstone when financial markets get choppy, uncertain, and outright scary. Stephen Covey wisely stated, "You have to decide what your highest priorities are and have the courage—pleasantly, smilingly, unapologetically—to say 'no' to other things. And the way to do this is to have a bigger 'yes' burning inside." The "no" is the intimidating and volatile bear market that might cause us to seek safety, such as hiding out in cash, while the thing that allows you to say "yes" to an ongoing process of saving and remaining invested is the dream.

The roots are the numbers—the monthly contribution you will need to make to meet a financial goal, the amount of risk you'll want to take along the way, and other practical features laid out in a financial plan. Every money goal comes with a cost, which can absolutely be planned for, but only after the wings have been firmly affixed.

A common problem I see is that investors start with the roots, causing so much initial drudgery that they never make it all the way to their dreams. Combining wings and roots sustains investor motivation, increasing the odds that goals can be achieved.

To experiment with this roots and wings approach, let's establish a goal together:

- **Set the vision**: Imagine having all the resources, time, and support needed to make your dreams come true. What is one aspiration you have always felt but haven't had the opportunity to pursue fully?
- **Align the goal with your values**: Reflect on the personal values and morals that this goal aligns with. The most meaningful ambitions are rooted in deeply held personal ethics and not fleeting pleasures.
- **Reverse engineer**: Start your goal-setting process by envisioning that you have already achieved your desired outcome. Then, work backward to identify the steps you took to get there. This approach breaks down your goals into manageable tasks, creating a clear roadmap to success. For instance, if your mission is to start an online venture, visualize yourself successfully running that business and then chart out the necessary steps to launch it, such as market research, product development, marketing strategies, and customer engagement. By reverse engineering, you will have a precise action plan to follow, making your goals more achievable.
- **Get granular**: Once you've reverse-engineered it, determine the roots of the goal, including the financial costs and other Type A details. Crunch all the numbers to gain a clear understanding of what it takes to bring your vision to life.
- **Get started**: Much like in physics, a behavior in motion tends to stay in motion, just as a behavior at rest tends to stay at rest. Automate as many parts of the process as possible and take action on the other aspects requiring effort on your end. Ready... BREAK!

It is so common for people to save and invest just because it's something we should do. Sure, it's great to see your net worth climb as you advance in your career and your investments grow over the years.

But what's the purpose? What's your responsibility beyond superficial numbers?

I don't have empowering words of wisdom for every reader's unique situation. Like Frankl, you must delve deep within yourself to discover your 'why'.

INVESTING, LIKE LIFE, IS UNCERTAIN (AND THAT'S OK)

IN A 1927 essay, H. P. Lovecraft, the man whose name is now synonymous with horror, wrote that "the oldest and strongest emotion of mankind is fear, and the oldest and strongest kind of fear is fear of the unknown."

This truth is embodied in an event in American history that is itself truly Lovecraftian: the Salem Witch Trials.

Uncertainty can lead us to seek certainty at any cost—even if the resulting actions are misguided. Consider the era of the trials. Settlers in that region during the late 17th century were members of a tight-knit Puritan community facing hard living conditions, constant threats from Native American tribes, and ongoing conflicts with neighboring communities. A deeply religious society, they placed high importance on the notion of maintaining a covenant with God and they valued, to a fault, moral purity. Puritan beliefs, along with a strict social hierarchy, commonly resulted in suspicion of anyone deviating from communal norms.

Mass hysteria soon broke out after unexplained illnesses and the peculiar behavior of some villagers. Those accused of witchcraft, largely based on hearsay, were swiftly put on trial. Legal procedures were sketchy at best; accounts were sometimes based on spectral evidence and witnesses' dreams. It was virtually impossible to prove one's innocence. Ultimately, a mere accusation of being a witch carried with it a social, and sometimes physical, death. The blaze of suspicion in Salem ran rampant.

In the search for certainty, 20 individuals were executed. As more people were charged with practicing witchcraft, it became like the Spiderman meme from social media, with one person pointing an accusatory finger at the other, and vice versa. Hysteria finally subdued once influential members of the town were accused of being witches themselves, and when the Massachusetts colonial government finally intervened.

The Salem Witch Trials demonstrate that our distaste for uncertainty is so great that we are compelled to fill that space with anything—no matter how destructive—to rid ourselves of the feeling of not knowing. This severe aversion to mystery extends beyond historical events; it's at the heart of many, if not most, types of mental illnesses, including panic attacks, generalized anxiety, and depression. A 2015 study found that uncertainty commonly drives Generalized Anxiety Disorder among those afflicted.[55] Some researchers even argue that distaste for uncertainty is the one fear to rule them all and that an ability to tolerate ambiguity is the sine qua non for maintaining a healthy mind.[56]

We dislike uncertainty so much that we hate it even more than bad news itself: Those undergoing a health crisis found their anxiety peaked not when receiving a life-changing diagnosis of something like cancer, but rather when waiting for the results of a biopsy. A cancer diagnosis, while certainly painful, at least provides a sense of direction and a roadmap for the next steps. Tom Petty was right: The waiting (and not knowing) really is the hardest part.

Since uncertainty is the root cause of much mental anguish and is the irritant in everything from a traffic jam to a medical scare, it's not surprising that it also impacts the way that we make decisions with our money.

According to a 2011 study in the journal *Behavior Therapy*, highly anxious individuals are willing to pay up to reduce the chance of uncertainty. In this analysis, bettors had the option to accept relatively unfavorable odds and lower monetary payouts in exchange for less time to stew on their wager's outcome. The results showed that participants with higher levels of intolerance for uncertainty were more likely to select immediacy, and the attendant financial loss.[57]

Within financial markets, uncertainty is the reason investors tend to flee for the perceived safety and certainty of cash during periods of turmoil. The 2008 Great Financial Crisis was a prime example. According to data from the Investment Company Institute (ICI), implied cash allocations surged from under 25% in late 2006 to nearly 50% around the stock market bottom in early 2009. While there is a degree of autocorrelation here (investors selling stocks and hiding in cash will cause the equity market to drop), once volatility begins to surface, a cascading flight to safety often ensues. As the S&P 500 recovered, that cash was gradually redeployed into risky assets.[58] History shows that people prefer the certainty of cash, even if it leads to dire consequences later in life.

Your task?

Control the controllables. Make regular contributions to your 401(k) and IRA, keep investment fees low, diversify across asset classes, and invest in yourself. Hiring a financial advisor is also commonly a worthwhile endeavor, as an advisor can guide you through volatile market periods and help you see blind spots in your financial plan (do you even have a plan?) as you progress through the various financial stages of life.

Your behavior is within your grasp, but politics, market returns, natural disasters, and so many more enigmatic factors are simply not. Worrying about such variables is futile.

Another easy win is to expand your time frame. As Ben Carlson points out, for a single calendar year, the S&P 500 has historically ranged from down 44% to up 53%. Widen out to a ten-year window, and average annual returns are confined to down 2% and up 20%. Over 30 years, things really get boring (but also beautiful for those staying the course); annualized returns vary modestly from up 8% to up 14%.[59] Finally, while it's basically a coin flip as to whether the S&P 500 will be higher or lower on any single session, there has never been a negative total return 20-year holding period in data from 1926 through 2022.

You must also know what to expect. Volatility, as Morgan Housel describes it, is like a ticket to the ballgame, or the price of admission to the investing playing field. Bear markets, corrections, and periods of protracted volatility are an inherent part of investing. Understanding that these fluctuations are a normal part of the market cycle can help alleviate the sting of surprise.

Since 1946, the S&P 500 has dropped 5% to 10% 84 times. A market-variety correction (a loss of 10% to 20%) happened 29 times. A standard bear market (a 20% to 40% decline) occurred nine separate times. Finally, a severe bear market crash of 40% or more took place on three occasions.[60] So, if you have, say, four decades to go as an investor, you should expect at least: 40 drops of 5–10% (one per year!); 15 falls of 10–20%; five standard bear markets (20–40% drop); and one or two severe crashes that will seem like the end of the world.

Even still, the S&P 500 has produced long-run returns that outpace cash, gold, corporate bonds, Treasurys, and real estate. The upshot is that knowing with certainty to expect uncertainty takes away some of the shock of constant surprises and can keep you in the investing game.

Lastly, take care of yourself. Investing in your mental and

emotional well-being is crucial when dealing with uncertainty. Practices like meditation, self-care, and stress management aid in maintaining a balanced mindset and making better decisions during shaky times. Be sure to also build and cultivate a support network and seek professional advice when needed. Avoid checking your account balances more than a few times a year. And finally, staying at arm's length from market news (noise) can also contribute to your overall well-being and financial resilience.

Learning to tame the power of uncertainty is a central part of leading a fulfilling life and achieving financial success. Life is inherently uncertain and acting otherwise means that we cut ourselves off from valuable experiences and the sort of risk that will allow us to compound our wealth. Making amends with chaos and unpredictability can lead to personal growth and long-term financial rewards as an investor. Just like getting lost in a spellbinding read or being tossed for a loop by a movie's plot twist, market unpredictability should not be feared, but welcomed and embraced.

MONEY CAN KINDA, SORTA BUY HAPPINESS SOMETIMES

WHAT IS THE *Great American Novel?* It's one of those conversations you have with friends after a few drinks, or perhaps pose to a first date as a barometer of compatibility. Sure to devolve into good-natured disagreement, it is the sort of question that is absolutely unanswerable and yet endlessly entertaining to discuss.

So, gentle reader, what's yours?

Is it *Moby Dick*, the tale of a monomaniacal sea captain, hell-bent on revenge? Or maybe it's *Uncle Tom's Cabin*, Harriet Beecher Stowe's gut-wrenching read on the horrors of slavery, outsold only by the Bible in the century in which it was released?

While these books, and many others, certainly have their claim to the throne, my vote goes to *The Great Gatsby* by F. Scott Fitzgerald.

As the story goes, Jay Gatsby seems to have it all. Except for the girl. Living a life of luxury, the charming man is in constant pursuit of Daisy Buchanan, but he remains an enigma to those close to him. Gatsby is one to throw extravagant parties and show off his valuable possessions, all while casting an aura of opulence in order to impress Daisy. He convinces himself that his wealth will deliver happiness and earn him Daisy's adoration.

Things don't go according to plan for Gatsby, though. He fails to find true happiness through material riches and by hosting lavish parties. Those decoys hide his true loneliness and unfulfilled desires. Indeed, he finds that money can neither buy back the past, nor connect him emotionally with Daisy.

As Penguin says of *Gatsby*:

> It nailed the unbridled hedonism of the Jazz Age perfectly and presciently. How, back then, was anyone to know the music was about to stop and the lights come up? That America would soon be left, empty flute in hand, stumbling about the sticky dancefloor of economic depression with no idea where to find the exit. Fitzgerald knew it. And *The Great Gatsby* proved to be his crystal ball: Nothing lasts forever… not even an American Dream.[61]

There are many reasons to love this novel. Its beautifully constructed prose takes a close look at a singular period in American economic and cultural history, yet the reader is left with a satisfying aftertaste of Schadenfreude that comes from watching Jay Gatsby come to ruin.

I think many of us can empathize with Jay. As the novel explores the emptiness that so often accompanies the pursuit of wealth, a key theme emerges—money alone cannot deliver contentment to the soul. Gatsby is relegated to an underlying feeling of hollowness, and it's a reminder to all of us that we need something more. Something deeper.

In 21st-century America, we are conflicted when it comes to our attitudes toward money and happiness. On the one hand, we love money and pursue it with breathless haste. Our brains get a little dopamine hit when we land a big bonus or see numbers on a spreadsheet increase. But on the other hand, most of us don't have as much of it as we would like and thus do not want to believe that it is core to living a happy life.

So, let me ask you another question: Is money able to buy happiness? (You might want to hold off on asking that one over appetizers on a first date.)

My answer: kind of.

In 2010, Daniel Kahneman and Angus Deaton did extensive research on the link between happiness and money, specifically digging into how much annual income is needed to effectively purchase pleasure. They broke out happiness into two categories: emotional well-being and life evaluation. Scanning more than 450,000 responses to a Gallup-Healthways Well-Being Index (a daily survey of 1,000 U.S. residents conducted by Gallup), it was determined that the two categories had different correlates. Emotional well-being is driven primarily by things such as the state of your health, how lonely you are, and whether you smoke. Life evaluation, meanwhile, is figured more by your income and education.

Life evaluation tended to rise steadily as income rose, according to the research. Emotional well-being, however, topped out at about $75,000 of annual income. Adjust that for inflation, and we're talking a smidge over $100,000 today. While money can be used to reduce the number of things you hate doing—say the laundry, or mowing your lawn—it fails to supply happiness. Having a low income tends to exacerbate the emotional trials that come with misfortunes such as divorce, bad health, and being alone.[62]

Academics and practitioners alike ate this study up (I'm sure Gatsby would've too). It got incredible coverage and was shared repeatedly by experts who wanted to drive home the point that money mattered up to a point, but once the basics of our life were met, it didn't matter much. That perspective hit a chord that resonated with many, including me, as it seemed to confirm our priors. It justified both the pursuit of and our collective disdain for money.

But it turns out that the reality is a little more complicated than, 'money doesn't buy happiness beyond 75k.'

First off, the way we measure something like 'happiness' matters a great deal. For example, in their work, Kahneman and Deaton divided happiness into two types of subjective well-being.

Second, it would appear that distinct groups of people are impacted differently by wealth with respect to happiness. Further research has been done on this nuanced topic. One adversarial collaboration, whereby Kahneman teamed with the University of Pennsylvania's Matthew Killingsworth and Professor Barbara Mellers, challenged the initial research, asserting that happiness for most people increases up to annual earnings of $500,000. Thirty percent of people even feel accelerated, not linear, happiness gains as income rises above $100,000. But there is a dark side. The researchers found that 15% of folks fall in the 'unhappy group', where the relationship between happiness and money breaks down once they've hit $100,000 in yearly income. For that minority, other negative life events or mental health challenges outweigh any added benefit a bigger salary can bring.[63]

Indeed, the latest evidence suggests something wealthy people may feel full well: Much of our happiness stems from things outside of wealth and even outside of our control.

A seminal 2005 paper revealed that contentment comes down to three factors of differing importance. The 'happiness pie chart', constructed by researchers Sonja Lyubomirsky, Kennon M. Sheldon, and David Schkade, outlines that 50% of our happiness is determined by our genes, 40% by our activities, and just 10% by our life circumstances.[64] Critics argue that 50% for genes and 10% for life circumstances may be underestimates and that the results of the authors' work may represent differences among people rather than individual contributions to happiness. Other research suggests that as much as 70–80% of observed differences in happiness levels are attributable to genetics.[65]

Let's make this more salient. Suppose a child with a predisposition toward sadness is born to a parent with a similar leaning. They are likely to be raised with not only those genes, but also in an environment that reflects the parent's own experiences and emotional tendencies. The mom or dad may unknowingly foster a life at home that reinforces or even exacerbates feelings of sadness, effectively transmitting pessimism or negative life attitudes to the child. This interplay between nature (genetic predisposition) and nurture (environmental upbringing) may lead to lifelong feelings of sadness that money will likely not be able to ameliorate.

Whether it's 50% or 70%, one thing is for sure: A great deal of our mood is contingent on things that are beyond our control.

Let's recap what we know:

- Money reliably buys the absence of misery, which is present at low levels of wealth.
- For many, money improves self-appraised subjective well-being up to very high levels of wealth.
- For some, no salary amount is adequate to lift them from the throes of sadness.
- The way we spend our money has a material impact on its ability to buy us contentment.

So, can money buy you happiness? Up to a point, maybe, kind of, unless you're part of a significant minority for whom money never moves the needle that much.

We all crave simple and certain answers, but the study of human nature tends to defy these. What we can say definitively is that money, in isolation, is not the panacea that we sometimes treat it as and that a meaningful life must account for, but not be governed by, its pursuit at all costs.

ANYTHING WORTH DOING IS RISKY

"**P**RETTY LOFTY GOAL, Herb."

"Well, Lou, that's why I want to pursue it."

The 1980 Winter Olympics in Lake Placid, New York is best known for the 'Miracle on Ice.' Coach Herb Brooks led a U.S. hockey team of inexperienced, mainly college-age players, most of whom were not even eligible to be called rookies. They took on the dominant and four-time reigning gold medal-winning team from the Soviet Union. To call it a David versus Goliath encounter was not hyperbole.

Hollywood's 2004 depiction, *Miracle*, is what my generation is familiar with, but Baby Boomers and their parents got to watch the semi-final match live with Al Michaels calling the game. Just surviving to the penultimate round was heroic in itself, but Brooks aimed to make history.

Brooks was chastised by his peers for taking an unusual approach and having such confidence in his plan. The coach ran his players hard in advance of and throughout the Winter Olympics. For the semi-final, he devised a bold game plan that included a risky approach. Rather than playing conservatively and trying to minimize mistakes against the daunting Soviets, he encouraged his youthful team to take aggressive, though calculated, risks.

It was a rough start for the Americans. The Soviets put the first goal on the scoreboard, but Team USA then squared it up. The two teams battled back and forth before the winning shot was finally slapped. Captain Mike Eruzione gave the home team the lead with a goal halfway through the final period. After the longest ten minutes of the young players' lives, the iconic call was made by Michaels, "Do you believe in miracles? Yes!"

It wasn't just a blessing from above that resulted in the triumphant victory for the good ole red, white, and blue. Brooks, veteran coach that he was, knew that a defensive and conservative strategy would not work against the Soviet Union, comprised of the world's top players. To have any chance at earning a seat at the gold-medal final, he had to motivate his players to play daringly, attacking the Soviets, and focus on being on the offensive. Brooks believed that this style was optimal so that momentum was maintained throughout all three periods. That fearlessness in the face of adversity proved right, and the underdogs earned victory, and then later gold.

Winning on the ice à la '80 Olympic Team has its parallels to achieving success with money and in life. It takes calculated risks and ambition to create the future you want to live.

First, we must identify what makes life meaningful. According to a 2021 Pew Research survey of 19,000 adults across 17 developed countries, careers and material well-being are among the most common factors that determine a purposeful life.[66] Thirty-eight percent of respondents cite family and children as most crucial, followed by occupation and career. Ranking toward the middle are freedom and independence, along with hobbies and recreation.

It's easy and even heart-warming to picture life with a loving family, a rewarding career, and relaxing weekend activities. That, along with Lassie and a white picket fence in the suburbs, is basically the American Dream. But you have to work for the American Dream—it is not served on a platter for any of us. Each of life's key elements that determine happiness and contentment requires a degree of risk-taking to achieve it.

One of the most perilous undertakings is tying the knot. Data from the National Center for Health Statistics, as reported by the American Psychological Association, show that it's tantamount to a coin flip as to whether newlyweds will make it to their 20th anniversary. Experts generally find that between 40% and 50% of all marriages result in divorce.[67] Those are lousy odds. And divorce may play a role in why happiness tends to be lowest during middle age.

And if you are risk averse, then you should forget about having kids. Those extra mouths to feed are sure to drain your wallet and bring home viruses. The Brookings Institute figured that the total cost of raising a child in America from birth to age 17 is north of $300,000.[68] Beyond the dollars and cents, it is estimated that more than 22 million adults in the U.S. have been targets of parental alienation—a situation in which a child is influenced or even manipulated to be hostile toward one of their parents due to ongoing spousal strife.[69]

While not all of us are married with children, we all face risks at work. Forty percent of employees are fired from a job during their lifetime.[70] Along with marital problems, caring for aging parents, and other responsibilities in mid-life, a sudden job loss often sparks heightened stress and a further drift from contentment. Gone are the days of working nine-to-five for 40 years and then retiring with a comfy pension. Today's employment situation is more cut-throat, and those in Gen Z may have upwards of 17 different jobs along their career journey.[71]

If you really seek to be the underdog, start a business. Data from the U.S. Bureau of Labor Statistics expose that about one-in-five startups fail in year one, while about half shutter after about two years. Just 25% survive 15 years or more.[72]

Let's say you marry your dream partner, have two awesome kids, and work a rewarding career. The odds are still stacked against you if you want to reach financial freedom sooner rather than later; just 2% of Americans are millionaires.[73] A 2023 survey by LendingClub found that the majority of the country, 60%, live paycheck to paycheck.[74] Even among high-income earners, about 40% live hand to mouth. So, while you might see your neighbor driving that brand-new Range Rover, there's a decent likelihood that they are struggling financially.

I could go on, but I think you get the picture. Every single meaningful relationship, venture, and goal you've ever pursued has involved a degree of risk. And the same is true of markets and investing.

Hitting millionaire status rarely comes overnight, or by scoring one monster income year. More often, someone earns financial success through decades of a stable and growing income, saving and investing a percentage of their salary, keeping fixed costs in check, and not falling into behavioral traps like keeping up with the Joneses.

When it comes to investing, you must be bold. Grab a chair in the Herb Brooks school of risk-taking. The common study by Brinson and Singer finds that 90% of the variance of someone's investment returns is attributable to asset allocation. Put simply, your decision to take more or less risk is the biggest driver of returns. Keeping too much in cash or being bashful by way of a big bond position may keep you from long-run financial success. The worst outcome is finding yourself without comfortable savings by late in the game. So, in a sense, being risk averse with your portfolio today could be the biggest real risk over the decades.

Still, like Coach Brooks, you must be an intelligent risk-taker and recognize what might trip you up on the slippery investment rink. Here's what that looks like:

- **Making smart money decisions**: The intelligent risk-taker isn't watching financial TV or reading up on the latest hot stocks. Wise money moves involve a high degree of humility and a low appetite for jumping on board investment fads. Regular contributions to a 401(k), IRA, and HSA, along with a rising savings rate and zero reliance on high-interest-rate debt, build a solid foundation.
- **Staying diversified**: Savvy risk-takers go with low-cost funds. They don't have the hubris to time the market. Rather, owning bits and pieces of capitalism through index funds or inexpensive active strategies that span the world of stocks stands the best chance of winning the financial freedom game.
- **Embracing patience**: Becoming a 401(k) millionaire happens over an unsatisfyingly long time. Year by year, it often feels like you're making little progress toward building wealth. Maintaining a long-term perspective, though, is critical.

Think about the most meaningful thing you have ever done. I would wager that it took a measure of risk, uncertainty, and hard work to achieve. In this, as with all risk, comes a valuable lesson: To strive for certainty is to doom oneself to mediocrity.

Consider the person who remains unattached to avoid risking heartache and finds loneliness in the process. Or the would-be entrepreneur who never makes the leap of faith and wastes a career working at jobs they hate. The irony of obsessive loss aversion is that our worst fears become realized in our attempts to manage them.

FOCUS ON
STRENGTHS

ALBERT EINSTEIN, THE epitome of genius, faced harsh judgments in his youth. Born in 1879, his formative years were not full of brilliance. He was called "stupid" by some, and language proficiency and social skills were areas in which he had trouble. Einstein struggled to read full sentences, causing a few of his elders to label him as "mentally deficient" or even "retarded."[75]

His slow progress in school prompted his parents to grow worried that their son lacked intellectual abilities. In the classroom, Einstein never truly conformed to the traditional education system, and his teachers often saw him as disruptive—not exactly one for the gifted program. Author Walter Isaacson wrote about Einstein even being expelled by one headmaster, who was convinced he would never make anything of himself.

Those early criticisms obviously failed to capture Einstein's intellectual prowess. In fact, some of these shortfalls turned out to foster his acumen, as slow verbal skills taught him to think in pictures. Said Isaacson, "[A young Einstein] thought, 'What would it take to be able to ride alongside a light beam?' And that led him to ultimately reject the notion of Newton—that time is constant."[76]

Think about that—the fact that Einstein couldn't speak until he was four years old became the catalyst for his talent to visualize complex concepts. These thought experiments laid the foundation for his later theories and revolutionary scientific research.

Einstein was also gifted in the sense that he didn't care about others' critiques. He found solace in his interests and progressively excelled in areas that piqued his curiosities; physics and math among them. Einstein later found himself in a more supportive environment, when he attended the Polytechnic Institute of Zurich, an institution that refined pupils' strengths. His professors quickly recognized his exceptional abilities in math and physics. The rest is science history.

Einstein's journey illustrates that locking into your strengths can lead to greatness. What's more, the very deficits that he was condemned for ended up being the wellspring of his brilliance. All it took for Einstein's true potential to emerge was a focus on his fortes instead of dwelling on his drawbacks.

When it comes to our financial lives, many of us tend to fixate on our flaws rather than hone our strengths. Numerous studies have highlighted this inclination. One survey found that 70% of Americans said that they were bad with money, with overspending their chief sin.[77] More in-depth research conducted by Morningstar trumpeted the fact that 98% of respondents claimed they had at least one money bias.[78] Maybe that's why the very thought of having to save more stirs up stress in our minds: The latest Stress in America study, performed by the American Psychology Association, found that 72% of us are worried about money in an unhealthy way.[79]

But are we really that hopeless? Well, there are a couple of reasons why we are more in touch with our deficits rather than our gifts.

First is *negativity bias*, which suggests that we are more likely to be affected by negative information and experiences than positive ones. The bias explains why bad first impressions are so hard to overcome, why we remember insults rather than praise, and why we are more attuned to negative news than feel-good news.

"If it bleeds, it leads," is a common media bent, but did you know that accusatory articles are more likely to be interpreted by readers as truthful than equivalent stories framed positively? Fiery, negative reports attract more viewers, and more attention often means greater validity, according to 2011 research by Benjamin E. Hilbig.[80]

Second, and even more cynically, Wall Street needs you to think that you're incompetent so that they can sell you their junk. In the same way that the beauty industrial complex preys on our fears of being unattractive (and therefore, unlovable), Wall Street depends on you believing that you're bad with money, so they can offer expensive products and services to address your perceived weaknesses.

Behavioral finance itself bears some guilt here. The study of humans' financial decision-making has largely mirrored the trajectory of the broader discipline of psychology in that it has focused on pathology first and has only lately come around to the study of wellness and wholeness. Psychology as a formal discipline began in 1854, but it was not until the late 1990s when 'positive psychology', the study of greatness and thriving rather than dysfunction and depravity, was launched. Similarly, behavioral finance began with the study of bias and 'irrationality', and has only more recently begun to emphasize how financial decisions can contribute to human thriving.

Now let's get practical. Typically, when we set a goal, it's about overcoming and white-knuckling our way past something we are not naturally good at. For example, if we need to lose some weight, then we set a goal to run five miles a day, even though we hate running. If we want to save more, then we create a punishing budget that deprives us of many of the things that we love.

What if I told you there was a better way built on positive psychology and behavioral finance concepts?

By leveraging our existing interests and strengths, we can increase the likelihood of sticking with our goals while finding joy in the process.

There's a psycho-babble term for this. *Hedonic motivation*, also known as pleasure-seeking motivation, intuitively asserts that we are naturally inclined to adopt habits that bring us happiness, satisfaction, and even a thrill, while avoiding behaviors that cause discomfort or pain.[81] For example, a 2003 study concluded that individuals are more likely to keep to an exercise regime when they simply like doing it.[82]

The parallels between health and wealth are many, and if hedonic motivation works for your workout routine, it can be practical for our personal finances too.

So, let's talk about some potential money strengths of yours, many of which will not appear overtly financial:

- **Strong community**: If you're a social butterfly, connect with a financial advisor who shares your values. If you are retired, share your money experiences with younger people.
- **A love of learning**: If you enjoy reading and researching, delve into some of the best personal finance books (you're here now, so you're off to a fantastic start on this).
- **Enjoyment of low-cost fun**: Learning to enjoy low-cost fun can be a saving and investing super-power. A walk through a historic neighborhood, window-shopping, hiking, cooking at home; all of these are cheap and rewarding. Use those saved bucks to build your portfolio, but also focus on how you'd like to spend your money on things that are worth it for you.

- **Employer who values you**: Rather than scrimp and save, perhaps your aim should be to grow your top line through a promotion at work. You can also mentor the millennials and Gen Zers on your team—that's a major corporate value add.
- **Attention to detail**: Apply your keen eyes to analyzing your budget, investment options, and critique your long-term financial plan so that you make better decisions now and tomorrow.
- **Ability to delay gratification**: It takes discipline to resist impulses. If you have this gift, you can use it to increase your savings rate, so you can invest more for the future.
- **Love of travel**: There are few more powerful uses of money to boost happiness than spending on new experiences. If traveling the world is your thing, you've got a leg up on soaking up the best life has to offer. Here's a tip: Try saving for your retirement by matching each dollar saved with a dollar for a big trip.
- **Entrepreneurial spirit**: Starting your own side hustle isn't a sure thing, but it's no coincidence that the average millionaire has multiple streams of income. Consider a side hustle that allows you to start small and iterate until you find a fit between what you do and what the market needs.
- **Negotiation skills**: Advocate for yourself across financial situations, including asking for a raise at work, or to land a bigger and better salary elsewhere.

The beauty here is in discovering how each of these strengths can naturally benefit your money life without much effort or pain. Some of them might even add a touch of fun to the process.

To get started, brainstorm a long list of all your strengths, talents, and blessings, and do not filter or judge any of your unique qualities. Next, identify an area in your financial life that could use some improvement or growth. Finally, explore how each of your strengths can be channeled to either move you closer to your desired money goals, or better align your money habits with your true values.

Remember, every strength you possess, no matter how seemingly unrelated to personal finance, has the potential to contribute to your financial well-being. Just as a delinquent child can become the world's greatest genius, your gifts can undoubtedly be put to good use on your money journey.

FAILURE CAN BE
THE BEST TEACHER

TRIAL AND ERROR is a stern instructor. We can read about
all the best tips and most effective methods to build wealth
over time, but true improvement for us fallible human beings often
requires slip-ups and getting dragged through the mud now and
then. Strength comes from realizing the error of our ways and
pressing forward with a new-found knowledge of what doesn't work.

Few pioneers in history personify that reality more than Thomas
Edison. While not known for his great wealth, the brilliant inventor
epitomized the notion that failure can be the best teacher. The
Midwestern visionary is renowned for developing breakthrough
products in electric power generation, communications, the motion
picture industry, and is best known for inventing the electric
lightbulb. But his journey to earning more than 1,000 patents was
riddled with failures.

One of Mr. Edison's inventions that was viewed as a major
swing and a miss at first blush was the nickel-iron alkaline storage
battery, also known as the Edison Battery. Intended to power
electric vehicles, Edison put countless hours and invested hefty
sums into the battery project, but there were technical problems

left and right. It simply struggled to keep up with other emerging battery technologies at the time.

The public ultimately viewed the project as a failure, but Edison took a different mental mindset. Rather than tossing the concept into the circular file, he considered his efforts as opportunities to learn and improve. The GOAT inventor in American lore famously quipped, "I have not failed 10,000 times—I've successfully found 10,000 ways that will not work." Edison *embraced the suck*, always confident that each screw-up offered valuable insights and knowledge that brought him closer to inevitable success.

After the Edison Battery's so-called disappointment, he shifted his focus to other breakthrough projects. The school of hard knocks taught him that there might be something more to develop in the electricity space. He would go on to invent the incandescent light bulb, propelling modern society into a new era; a development that arguably wouldn't have come had he not failed in his battery endeavor.

Failure to Edison was simply a step in the scientific process. His ability to learn from what didn't work, adapt, and persevere led to his proclivity to innovate. What must have been grueling from a psychological perspective, however, was hearing others constantly talk about his failures almost like they were supposed to be personal defeats. Societal pressures can take their toll and it sometimes takes a high degree of social indifference to forge ahead.

———

There is so much we can take away here from a financial perspective. Not only is brilliance seen in Edison's inventions but also in his mental fortitude, perhaps even audacity, to ignore the naysayers and nonbelievers. His life should also instill in us that, to quote the man again, "Many of life's failures are people who did not realize how close they were to success when they gave up."

Let's face it, you and I are no Edison, but we can empathize with him when it comes to our paths toward success with money. Financial setbacks will happen, and we might even catch serious flak from friends and family. The trick is to put on our Edison hats and consider failures as valuable lessons and useful speedbumps along our money journey.

The truth is that failure is not innately good or bad; it is only as good or as bad as our attitude and mindset. Researchers at Northwestern University deem failure as "the essential prerequisite for success" in a 2019 paper that analyzed more than 700,000 grant applications submitted to the National Institutes of Health from 1985 to 2015. Their review of 46 years' worth of venture capital startup investments drew a similar conclusion; there is no success without a period of disappointment.[83]

When the research team aimed to create a model that could reliably predict success, they found that "every winner begins as a loser." It turned out that scientists and venture capitalists who eventually landed on a winner had failed about the same number of times as those who failed and gave up.

Failure was not the grand differentiator!

What separated the winners from the losers was learning from mistakes, figuring out what worked and what didn't, and adjusting from there. The 'failure' group generally came up empty when it came to identifying lessons, whereas the successful group made effective tweaks and took action.

The upshot: It's not about mindlessly repeating the same actions, but rather failing fast in a smart way, adapting, then improving. Edison could vouch for that.

———————

So, what do we know about failure?

It is inevitable, and winning ideas almost always begin as duds. We also know that nothing about defeat is noble in and of itself, but rather it's only as useful as our approach to it and our commitment to learning from it. Once again, unfortunately, our brains tend to get in the way, causing us to not learn as much from failure as we ought to.

We often struggle to grow from errors and defeats, and we under learn from mistakes. That was one of the conclusions from work done by researchers Lauren Eskreis-Winkler and Ayelet Fishbach who developed the Facing Failure game.[84] The experimental game consisted of successive rounds of multiple-choice questions, and feedback from earlier rounds was given to help participants perform better in later rounds. The more questions answered correctly, the more money contestants earned. Thus, there was a financial incentive to learn from mistakes.

Here's where people went off the rails. Rather than figuring out what they did wrong and why, participants generally bypassed the sometimes cold and always truthful feedback. "Even when participants had the chance to earn a learning bonus that was 900% larger than the participation payment, players learned less from failure than success," the researchers wrote.

This behavior is seen in many other studies, too. It's known as the 'ostrich effect', and it describes our inclination to avoid negative information (even if it helps us improve).[85]

This phenomenon plays out very clearly when monitoring investor behavior. People stop checking their portfolios during bear markets since it relays bad news, but we are wont to compulsively tally our trades in bull markets.

The study concluded by offering up some help to combat our fight or flight response and other emotional biases. Their research found that it helps to observe others' failures—which provides a better perspective through self-distancing, allowing us to reframe failures as inspirational growth stories. Likewise, recognizing successes, feeling disappointment, and focusing on long-term goals are tips for staying on track and turning failure into fuel for growth.

We can apply all of these methods to our money because, just as in grant writing and venture capital, we know that blunders and losses are part of the game. Expect them. Just look at the stock market's history—along with being maybe the best vehicle for wealth accumulation in existence, the S&P 500 has declined 20% or more during 26% of all years since 1928, according to data put together by Ben Carlson.[86] In the short term, the chances of seeing red on the financial TV screen when the closing bell rings on any given session is about 45%. Trying to avoid those down days only makes it worse—so much so that roughly 80% of all day traders call it quits within two years.[87]

Instead of being overcome by failure, here's what I want you to do: Picture a recent financial mishap, or perhaps one that has always lingered in your mind. Now, approach it with this framework:

- **Acknowledge**: Recognize and accept that things did not turn out the way you planned.
- **Reflect**: Analyze the situation, understand what went wrong, and why. Don't be afraid to think about the negative consequences of what took place.
- **Seek feedback**: Gather insights and advice from experts or trusted sources. Friends and family can help, but make sure their guidance is grounded in evidence.
- **Identify lessons**: Extract key takeaways from the experience just as Edison would have done. Where did things go wrong? What can be done next time to help ensure it doesn't happen again?
- **Make adjustments**: Here is where the scientific method can shine. Figure out how to go about it differently next time.

- **Take action**: Apply the lessons learned and make proactive choices to enhance financial well-being, appreciating the failure for what it truly was—a helpful stepping stone.

Instead of being discouraged by failure, adopting a structured approach to learn from financial flubs might just reinvent and reinvigorate your relationship with money.

Class dismissed.

YOUR LIFE WILL BE AS RICH AS YOUR FRIENDS

THE ULTIMATE SIGN of branding success is when a company or its main product becomes so ubiquitous that the name comes to represent the whole category.

Here's what I mean: We don't consult a search engine with a question. We google it. I would never ask for a facial tissue when I have a cold. I'd request a Kleenex. If I asked my Jell-O-loving kids if they wanted some gelatin for dessert, I doubt they would even know what I was talking about. And when it comes to owning the category for signatures, it's John Hancock.

But how is it that Hancock's handle became synonymous with signatures? The story is fascinating and demonstrates the power of social proof to change life for the better or worse.

The 56 delegates to ink their names on the Declaration of Independence knew they were signing their death certificates if events did not go as they planned. This reality was crystalized in the document itself, which reads: "And for the support of this Declaration, with a firm reliance on the protection of divine

Providence, we mutually pledge to each other our Lives, our Fortunes and our sacred Honor."

They were willing to die for it—and to lose all their money, too.

Social proof played a key role in the 13 colonies breaking away from British Rule in 1776. The psychological phenomenon suggests that if we see other people behaving a certain way, we are more likely to do the same—our brains find validation in actions observed. John Hancock, president of the Continental Congress and first signatory of the Declaration, took it upon himself to use the bias to his advantage. Leading off by conspicuously signing his name big and bold, he was putting his neck particularly on the line and telegraphing confidence to other delegates yet to sign. The act served as social proof for the other signees in the room that Hancock meant business. And it worked.

His peers felt reassured. They were influenced by Hancock and felt more confident that they were making the right decision. One by one, others stepped forward to affix their names to the document. The social proof cast by Hancock's famous signature established a sense of unity and solidarity among the other 55 delegates, fortifying their resolve and unwavering stance for independence. The people of the 13 colonies were likewise inspired, and the international community took notice.

Social proof works because we are tribal and social beings. It's an evolutionary truth that allows us to build great cultures and civilizations, but it also means that we are greatly influenced by the behavior of those around us, for better or worse.

A 2007 paper by Nicholas A. Christakis and James H. Fowler, using the data set from the Framingham Heart Study, one of the largest and longest-running health studies ever performed, concluded that one of the best predictors of obesity was whether people in ones' immediate circle became obese, even when controlling for other important variables. The researchers analyzed the potential person-to-person spread of being drastically overweight as a factor in the worsening epidemic. The results suggested that just having a friend who became overweight increased an individual's likelihood of becoming obese themselves by 57%. If you have a sibling who recently put on significant weight, you are 40% more likely to follow suit. Similarly, if one spouse turned obese, the likelihood of the other spouse becoming obese increased by 37%.[88] Clearly, social factors play a significant role in our health.

Social proof can also work wonders for children and adolescents facing various challenges in their lives. Big Brothers Big Sisters is a well-known nonprofit that operates mentoring programs for young people in the U.S. and Canada. Research conducted in 1998 found that youths with a positive mentor showed higher levels of education and economic self-sufficiency. Children aged 10 to 16 who had a mentor were much less wont to later use illegal drugs, hit someone, or skip school compared to a control group. Being around a positive elder had benefits at home, as well. They got along better with family members and were generally more confident as young adults.[89]

And it shouldn't surprise you that what works in the gym and the playground also plays out in the workplace. The influence of corporate social networks on corporate performance was starkly illustrated by the study, "Corporate Social Capital and Liability." Individuals embedded in circles with high levels of social capital, characterized by trust, information sharing, and collaboration, were more likely to then access valuable resources, such as financial capital and business opportunities, leading to better financial outcomes.

But just as surely as social proof can increase prosocial behavior and workplace performance, it can also lead to unintended negative consequences. One such consequence is the Werther-Effect, which describes the phenomenon of copycat suicide behavior prompted by the media's reporting. The effect underscores the potential influence on vulnerable individuals, who may be more susceptible to suicidal thoughts and behaviors when exposed to detailed or sensationalized depictions of suicide.

The study, "The 'Werther-Effect': Legend or Reality?" was published in 2007 and shed light on the power of social proof. The research describes a set of media guidelines for reporting on suicides that were introduced in Austria as an experimental suicide prevention measure starting in 1987. The guidelines serve as a framework for news outlets to report on self-harm-related topics responsibly and sensitively, aiming to minimize the risk of triggering copycat suicides.

The results of the implementation were significant. The initial impact of the new media guidelines was notably positive, with an 80% reduction in subway suicides and attempted suicides within six months of implementation. More broadly, the new, more sensitive media reporting guidelines successfully influenced individuals' behavior, as evidenced by a 40% decrease in deaths by suicide in Vienna compared to the mid-1980s, prior to the implementation of the guidelines. These trends suggest that the Austrian media guidelines had a positive impact on suicidal behavior.[90]

Looking specifically at the significance of our friends, it has become common wisdom that who we are is determined to a large extent by our five closest pals. Choose wisely, dear readers. In a follow-up study to the Christakis and Fowler obesity research cited earlier, the pair concluded that if you have a friend who smokes, then you are 61% more likely to be a smoker yourself. Furthermore, if a friend of a friend smokes, the subjects are 29% more likely to smoke, and the risk increases by 11% for contacts at the third degree of separation.[91]

On the other hand, the study also revealed that happiness can be contagious within social networks. If a friend of a friend of a friend is happy with their life, it can increase an individual's likelihood of being happy by about 6%.[92] Believing ourselves to be solitary and self-determined, we dramatically underestimate the power of social networks to encourage us to be healthy, happy, and yes, wealthy.

Our social nature is what allows us to cooperate in ways unthinkable in the rest of the animal kingdom, but it also means that we are often as good, as bad, as happy, or as sad, as the people we surround ourselves with. Upon recognizing the power of social proof and social contagion on our overall health, wealth, and happiness, it becomes essential for those seeking a fulfilling and prosperous life to be mindful of their choice of friends. In return, it is equally important that we embody the qualities of a supportive and uplifting friend who can positively influence others along the way, setting in motion a virtuous cycle with far-reaching positive impacts.

SHOW ME YOUR BUDGET AND I'LL SHOW YOU YOUR VALUES

H OW MUCH DO you like dolphins? Rate it on a scale from 1 to 10. If you're like most folks, I bet you're in the 8 to 10 range, right? I mean, the vast intelligence, the graceful water acrobatics, the cute bottle nose. What's not to like?

But let's move beyond superficialities and assess the extent of your true affinity for dolphins by looking at your behavior:

- When was the last time you drew a dolphin?
- Have you recently given any money to a dolphin rescue initiative?
- Have you spent any quality time with a dolphin recently—perhaps joining one of your favorite ocean companions for a swim?
- Did you, in the last month, speak with any of your friends about dolphins?

Gee, it seems like you may not care about dolphins as much as you thought.

In a former professional life, I was tasked with interviewing bank executives pre-hire to determine their level of fit within an organization. When I asked applicants why they were applying for the job in question, the answer was, almost inevitably, "I'm passionate about this work." This answer was so common (and to me, so unbelievable) that I followed up with, "Wonderful. What evidence is there of this passion in how you spend your time?" A question that was met with many frustrated stares and pregnant pauses.

You see, passion leaves a trace. The best evidence of loving your family is not your insistence of the same, it's the time you spend with them. Similarly, looking at your personal budget is the ultimate arbiter of what you say you value versus what you actually treasure in life.

Let me beat you up a little bit more before we get into why this is and what you can do to align your money with what and who you hold closest to your heart.

We all would claim to prize our health, but our behavior tells a different story. According to the CDC, more than one-in-three of us eat fast food on any given day.[93] A study from 2014 found that the typical American spent $1,200 annually on fast food. Adjusted for inflation, that number is probably closer to $1,600 today. Adding insult to injury, the study only looked at a 50-week period, so tack on a few more bucks (and a few more pounds to the collective waistline) for a 52-week year. We may claim that a healthy diet is who we are, but data on people's real spending paints a different picture.

Red-blooded Americans also say they value work-life balance and understand the importance of getting away from the hustle and bustle of the nine-to-five grind. A Pew survey revealed that 89% of workers said it was 'extremely' or 'very' important that their employer provide them ample paid time off.[94] And yet we leave an average of 9.5 PTO days on the table each year.[95]

Are we all just a bunch of no-good liars? Or is there something deeper going on here?

The reality is both men and women, young and old, wealthy and indigent, all have issues matching spending and saving with what we profess to value. The bottom line is that the way we allocate our money reflects our true priorities. To slightly misquote Jay Z, "Men lie, women lie, budgets don't lie."

The existence of this apparent behavioral flaw can be traced back to what psychologists refer to as the fundamental attribution error (FAE). It's a cognitive bias that leads individuals to attribute another's actions to internal factors while attributing their own behavior to external factors. Put another way, we take credit for success and blame others for our failures and flaws.

The analogy I like to use is when you're rushing home from work on a hectic commute. Suppose some reckless soul impulsively cuts you off on the highway—it's easy to label that driver as rotten to the core, ignoring any situational variables. But when you, in a moment of haste, inadvertently follow too close or even intentionally speed—it's just because you want to get home to your family.

The FAE highlights how we tend to assess others based on their actions, but evaluate ourselves (often in an unrealistically positive light) based on a self-serving mashup of our best wishes. But that's the thing—life does not reward you for your intentions. It rewards you for what you do, and your budget is a clear indication of what you're up to.

It's because of blind spots like this that others may know us better than ourselves. Studies performed on the FAE underscore that individuals frequently manipulate their perception of reality to align with their self-image.[96] But there is someone else lurking that knows us best of all (and it's within reaching distance)—our checkbooks.

So, do me a favor: Pick your top three values. If you are unsure what they might be, there are online resources and apps that help. I personally like the Core Values List compiled by James Clear. Rank your top three and then pull up your budget or credit card statement from last month. You are about to enter the financial confessional.

- If you say you value spirituality, are you tithing or giving to charitable causes?
- If you say you value personal growth, are you going to therapy, or investing in further education?
- If you say you cherish your kids, did you take off enough days from work to spend quality time with them before they grow up?

Odds are, you've lied to yourself to some extent about your identity and values. We all do it!

Looking at yourself through the lens of your spending habits offers a fast and genuine reflection of your true self and points us to real opportunities for self-improvement.

MAKE GOOD EASY,
MAKE BAD HARD

M ANY LAWS, TAX rules, and regulations require us to jump through hoops and hire Ph.D.s and attorneys just to understand what we need to do or not do to please our government overlords. But some of the most successful public policies are rooted in simplicity and clarity, playing on our inclination to be lazy.

The Behavioral Insights Team (BIT), also known unofficially as the Nudge Unit, has achieved significant accomplishments by incorporating behavioral science into government directives. Through the skillful application of behavioral science, the global social purpose organization formed in 2010 has improved tax compliance, championed healthy behaviors, enhanced pension enrollment and retirement savings, enacted education reform, and continues to address flaws in the criminal justice system, including focusing on the rehabilitation of inmates.

A common thread throughout BIT's many successful initiatives is the idea that making things easier leads to an increase in a desired behavior. In contrast to the intimidating and complex language used in IRS letters, the Nudge Unit utilizes personalized and simple messaging, resulting in improved compliance and increased tax revenue collection. In terms of a healthier society, clearer nutrition labels designed by the team along with impactful warnings that underscore the dangers of smoking have resulted in healthier food choices by families and higher quit rates among smokers. On the financial front, BIT's work on simplifying retirement plan enrollment continues to draw workers to save for the future. Simplified goal setting, peer support, and personalized messaging have had a profound impact on pupils, enhancing student performance. Finally, behavioral insights and interventions in the criminal justice system have resulted in lower levels of prison recidivism.

While the behaviors the Nudge Unit has been tasked with solving for are diverse and wide-ranging, a single model sits behind much of their success: A widely applicable model known as the EAST framework. EAST is an easily remembered acronym that stands for Easy, Attractive, Social, and Timely.

"The behavioural science literature can be complex, so having a simple framework which policymakers can easily access and apply is invaluable. As the Minister responsible for Government Policy, I've seen how some of these insights can be applied in practice to help generate policy that's smarter, simpler and is highly cost-effective," said Oliver Letwin, former minister for government policy in the UK.[97]

While all four elements of EAST are impactful, I'd like to focus here on the 'E', which is all about making good behavior easy and bad behavior hard. Perhaps the most impactful example of this is the Save More Tomorrow (SMT) program developed by Richard Thaler and Shlomo Benartzi in the late 1990s. The initiative aimed to address the issue of Americans' low retirement savings rates by leveraging behavioral insights to nudge workers into saving more for their future.

But that's hard for many people due to present bias—the tendency of people to give stronger weight to rewards that are more immediate. While there are some supersavers out there, most of us prefer to enjoy today, including the fruits of our labor, and leave worrying about the future for another time. As a result, procrastination and inertia commonly result in low retirement plan contribution rates.

To overcome the psychological barriers, the SMT program was introduced, guided by the behavioral expertise of Thaler and Benartzi. It was a voluntary plan, allowing employees to commit to increasing their future contributions, often tied to their annual raise. Individuals were auto-enrolled, and they had the option to opt out at any time. These may seem like minor details, but the concept of commitment and the auto-enrollment feature help mitigate the inertia bias mentioned before. It made saving easy. Also, linking a contribution rate increase to annual salary bumps alleviates the pain a worker might feel when seeing a smaller take-home pay amount. From then on, how much a person defers to the plan goes up with each subsequent raise until a preset max is hit.

Did it work? I'd say so!

According to data from the University of Chicago Booth School of Business, the average saving rates for SMT participants more than tripled, from 3.5% to 11.6%, over the course of just 28 months.[98] Other studies back up Booth's findings. The upshot is that by taking advantage (in a constructive way) of our behavioral biases, policymakers can prompt (or nudge) people to easily make better decisions while still allowing them the freedom to make their own choices.

The SMT program is a notable example, but it is certainly not the only instance of how making good easy and bad hard can powerfully impact our behavior.

James Clear, in his book *Atomic Habits*, asserts that laying out your gym clothes and placing your running shoes by the door increases the chances that you will go for a morning run. This practical trick removes barriers and uses the commitment technique to help get some cardio in, making exercise just a little easier.

Now let's say you ran a few miles at sun-up. By midday you might be famished, so you arrive at the work cafeteria. Something's different, though. At the front of the line, there are fruits, then vegetables, then some protein. In Richard Thaler and Cass Sunstein's classic book *Nudge*, it was shown that arranging more nutritious options earlier in the cafeteria lines (making it easier to fill up your plate with real food) can get people to eat healthier. The simple act of making it easier to grab fruits and veggies led to a 30% uptick in loading up on healthy food.

Staying on the topic of food, a 2017 paper, "Contribution of snacks to dietary intakes of young children in the United States," found junk snacks account for 28% of children's overall energy intake, partially because they are so convenient.[99] One way you can make good easy and bad hard is to focus on buying healthy snacks at the grocery store and ensuring that junk food does not make it into your house in the first place. Research on college students found that, among other factors, having easy access to sweet and salty options meant that they loaded up on unhealthy foods.[100] By replacing chips, crackers, and cookies in your shopping cart with carrots, cashews, and chia seeds, you'll make it easier to eat better. The research is clear that we are what we eat and we tend to eat what's around.

After a long day at work, you get home and ask your spouse where they want to go for dinner. You land on one of your go-to restaurants. Lately, along with making it a habit to run in the morning, you have been trying to rein in your spending. With this goal in mind, you might want to hide your credit card and reach for some cash. Research from Dan Ariely suggests that we tend to spend less when doling out dollar bills rather than conveniently swiping, inserting, or tapping with a credit card. After all, that swipe is so easy that it hardly seems real! By using cash instead of credit, you are making it harder to do the thing you're trying to avoid, overspending.

———————————

All too often we are prone to grand gestures in our efforts to make good financial habits stick, but as SMT and other research prove, sometimes the best thing we can do is to make things easy.

Here's a challenge: Before moving on to the next chapter, commit to one action that will either make a good financial behavior easier, or a bad behavior harder.

Need some inspiration? Here are some ideas:

- **Automate investments**: Take a cue from the SMT program and increase your investment contributions through your 401(k) plan's auto-increase or auto-escalation feature. If you already have that knocked out, check with your brokerage firm to see if you can automatically move money periodically from your checking account into an IRA and have it invested. The fewer logins and clicks needed to invest more, the better off you will be.
- **Simplify your finances**: Reduce the number of credit cards you use, consolidate investment accounts, and establish clear spending categories to see where your money is going out the door. Ultimately, you can reduce stress, save time, and improve your money awareness with simpler financial processes.
- **App overload**: How many apps on your phone end up draining cash from your virtual wallet? Maybe it's a shopping site or a sports betting outlet. Splurges here or there and the occasional weekend wager is all fun and games, but for some people, the ease with which they can spend and gamble with just a few swipes is too costly. Consider simply deleting those apps.

Making better money decisions doesn't require Herculean effort. All it takes is a few seemingly minor actions that set you up to adopt healthy and lucrative habits. It's all about removing barriers—physical and mental—that prevent us from making good decisions while establishing helpful walls to prevent bad behavior.

DELAYED GRATIFICATION IS THE ULTIMATE LIFE HACK

THE 13 DAYS of the Cuban Missile Crisis in October 1962 were among the most tense in United States history. The confrontation between the U.S. and the Soviet Union nearly escalated into a mutually assured nuclear disaster. It all started when it was discovered that the Soviets were covertly positioning missiles in Cuba, a mere 90 miles off the U.S. mainland.

President Kennedy had two choices: (1) Launch an immediate strike that would have cost many lives and even put the homeland in danger; or (2) pursue a diplomatic solution that would take time and a bit of finessing on the global stage. The latter option was also fraught with potential peril—waiting meant uncertainty about how the Soviet Union would respond. With bated breath, the world watched as the standoff ensued.

Kennedy kept his cool and sought the diplomatic route. In secret, he engaged Soviet Leader, Nikita Khrushchev, in resolution talks, all while instructing a naval blockade to be placed around Cuba to prevent further Soviet missile shipments to the island.

Waiting and thoughtfully considering all options paid off. A resolution came on October 28, 1962, when Khrushchev agreed to dismantle its missile installations in Cuba while the U.S. pledged not to invade the island nation.

Defusing the Cuban Missile Crisis required something we all often hate to do: waiting. The uncertainty that coincides with major world events—and significant forks in the road in our own lives—sometimes feels worse than whatever the outcome might be. For President Kennedy, remaining calm and not jumping into a military response proved to be the better tactic. Exercising patience enabled him to think with greater clarity, leading to the implementation of a more effective long-run strategy.

Shortly after the Cuban Missile Crisis, albeit with less at stake, The Beatles were faced with a similar conundrum. In the early 1960s, The Beatles had burst onto the pop music scene. The energy of John, Paul, George, and Ringo drew in thousands of young fans when on tour. In 1966, after a few years of wooing audiences with their catchy tunes, the group decided to pause live events and hit the studio to work on a new album.

That marked a pivotal moment in the band's evolution and the music industry writ large. Surely, they could have continued to earn massive paychecks performing in front of live audiences night after night all around the world. But it was by forgoing immediate financial success and increased popularity through the endorphin rush of live performances that the band took their sound to the next level. Within the serene confines of a studio, they had the opportunity to refine their craft and unleash their creativity through experimentation.

Over the ensuing years, The Beatles released their most renowned albums: *Revolver* (1966), *Sgt. Pepper's Lonely Hearts Club Band* (1967), and *The White Album* (1968). These edgy albums reshaped pop music and introduced new production methods, musical styles, and creative lyrics.

Financial success came, but not instantaneously. It was only after taking time out to level set where the group wanted to go next on their musical journey that benefits were reaped. Four young guys at the peak of success must have been tempted to keep doing what they were doing, snagging short-term rewards and being thronged by fans at sold-out events, but their thoughtful pursuit of new, challenging styles secured their place in music history. All they needed was love... and delayed gratification.

Both President Kennedy and The Beatles countered our usual human tendency to privilege today over tomorrow. The Immediacy Effect can plague us as investors if we aren't careful. In his book *Predictably Irrational*, Dan Ariely talks about Adam and Eve, stating, "You can ask yourself how many of us would sacrifice eternity in the Garden of Eden for an apple? Well, it turns out we do it, and we do it all the time."

Immediacy impacts how we handle money, too. Research finds that individuals donate more to victims of recent disasters as opposed to calamities that had a larger, but more distant impact. The upshot is that the brain's stimuli elicit immediate emotional signals in the aftermath of major catastrophes. When salience is high, the vividness of how we recall disasters causes us to think and act in the here and now.

But no study has entered the public consciousness as much as the Marshmallow Experiment. This coup de grâce example underscoring the benefits of delayed gratification has undoubtedly been told at countless financial advisor meeting rooms over the years.

Here's how it played out.

Psychologist and Stanford Professor Walter Mischel aimed to understand when self-control developed in children. The experiments, which began in the 1960s, involved offering a child one small immediate reward, or two small rewards if they waited 15 minutes. If the child did not succumb to temptation by gobbling up the single marshmallow, then they were rewarded with either a second marshmallow or a pretzel. During the 15-minute window, footage of the children demonstrates how hard it was for them to not devour the sweet marshmallow. They were jittery and anxious. Some eventually gave in to temptation, while others were successful in holding off until the researcher re-entered the room.

Years down the line, it was found that the preschoolers who delayed gratification scored better on SAT exams, achieved more academic accolades, and even had lower obesity levels compared to those who immediately scarfed down the single marshmallow. New research on the Marshmallow Experiment suggests that socioeconomic factors play a critical role in how individuals perceive resources (like food) and trust in authority (the experimenter). So, while there's nuance to the sources of strength around delayed gratification, the fact that it is powerful remains unquestioned.

———————

What does all of this have to do with your money?

Psychologically, we perceive saving money and investing—the very core behaviors of wealth-building—as a present loss. Moreover, stashing cash away for the future has about the same impact within our minds as setting money on fire. Bypassing the thrill of acquiring new things or enjoying a fun activity now in lieu of some hazy future upside simply feels lousy.

The thing is, delayed gratification is a skeleton key that unlocks almost every door leading to a better life—if you can delay gratification in one area of your life, you can do it with money too.

Yoon Lee, Ph.D., associate professor at Utah State University, found that adults who forgo unhealthy foods are also better with their money.[101] "When individuals consciously choose healthier options in their daily lives, they also tend to make better choices when it comes to making financial decisions," said Lee. The study revealed that individuals with higher (i.e., unhealthier) body mass index levels earned less household income and had a lower net worth.

The trick to practicing delayed gratification is to make it habitual and incorporate the concept into your life each day. While hitting the snooze button will always feel better than getting up and going for a run at zero-dark thirty, we know that regular physical activity is among the most beneficial actions we can take to improve brain health, keep our weight in check as we age, reduce the risk of disease, and strengthen our bones and muscles, according to the U.S. CDC.[102]

Now, let's apply that mindset and action to our relationship with money. While spending today on a thing is always going to feel better in the moment rather than socking it away for tomorrow, we know that our future selves will thank us for it. Robbing yourself now is a worthwhile and noble heist. Jacquette M. Timmons, a financial behaviorist based in Brooklyn, New York, says that there's a "feel-good connection" in the power of saving. "It boosts your confidence that you are prepared for the future," says Timmons. Just putting cold hard dollars to that concept tells the tale: Investing an extra $100 a month for 30 years at an 8% annual return pockets someone an extra $150,000 in retirement. Who wouldn't feel better about that?[103]

What's also great about consistently delaying gratification in your life is that it makes those moments of immediate pleasure even better. Research shows that splurges, whether financial or culinary, have a more positive impact when they are infrequent. Want that cookie to taste sweeter or the glow of that new purchase to last longer? Make it an event and not a habit.

Denying yourself the modicum of pleasure today has widespread benefits that will make you happier, healthier, and richer. The cherry on top is that making delayed gratification part of who you are adds a touch of delight to the occasional splurge.

UNLEARNING IS PART OF YOUR MONEY JOURNEY

W HO ARE YOU closest to in your family? Maybe a sibling near in age, or a cousin you have bonded with since childhood?

No matter how connected you may be with this person, chances are that as you have aged, you have increasingly gone your separate ways and now you reconvene mostly for special occasions. That's the way life goes with families and with friends.

But that's not how it went for the Eriksson sisters.

Ursula Eriksson and Sabina Eriksson are twins who garnered national notoriety in the United Kingdom beginning in May 2008. Inseparable, the ladies from Sweden embarked on a journey from Ireland to London that included a series of strange and tragic events.

Upon arrival in Liverpool, the sisters exhibited bizarre behavior, causing a fright among fellow travelers. Once on board a bus to London, their disturbances escalated, and reports say the driver was forced to pull over and fetch the police due to their disruptive behavior. No arrests were made, but the twins were not allowed back on the bus.

Subsequently, Ursula and Sabina were seen wandering near the busy M6 highway. They then inexplicably ran onto the busy road. The police were called to assist the women, but the two darted right and left through oncoming traffic. Ursula managed to evade the fast-moving vehicles, but Sabina was unfortunately struck, although her injuries were not severe.

Law enforcement arrived on the scene, only to witness the twins once again recklessly run onto the highway, resulting in another collision. This time, Ursula suffered serious injuries while Sabina, still in a coherent state, resorted to attacking a police officer before her subsequent arrest. Both sisters were rushed to the hospital, leaving bystanders concerned and bewildered as to what had just transpired.

Five hours after the incident on the M6, Sabina was discharged from the hospital and taken into custody. A court later sentenced the woman to a single day in prison after she pleaded guilty. Having already spent a night behind bars, she was released without a psychiatric evaluation. A free woman, Sabina wandered the streets in search of Ursula, but her actions soon took a sinister turn when she murdered a good Samaritan who had taken her in out of concern. While Ursula returned to Sweden after recovering, Sabina was sentenced to five years in prison, with the murder being the result of mental illness, according to the presiding judge.

Media attention on the case was intense, and speculation grew about what possible factors may have triggered the harrowing series of events. The sisters' friends and family were said to have described them as normal and friendly individuals with no clear indications of substance abuse or past criminal activity.

In court, the defense presented a case for folie à deux, literally 'madness of the two', or shared psychosis, as it is more commonly known.

In folie à deux, a healthy family member can become mentally ill by taking on the delusions of another family member by proxy. The distorted worldview of one mentally ill individual can spread through a sort of contagion, causing the other to view life through the same warped lens. The tragedy of the Eriksson sisters is an extreme illustration of this condition.

As I explain in *The Behavioral Investor*, our ability to empathize with, cooperate with, and even mirror the behavior of those with whom we are close is perhaps the pinnacle of human achievement. But if we uncritically swallow the worldview of those with whom we interact most frequently, it can also cause us to adopt some approaches to life and money that are harmful.

The most obvious and often innocuous example of folie à deux when it comes to financial behavior is how much we are influenced by our parents. Most adult children acknowledge that their mothers and fathers have had the most impact on their attitudes toward money, though research has found that explicit conversations about how to think about money often never took place.[104] The implication here is that financial attitudes are passed along observationally, but with limited insight into where they came from or how appropriate they are.

Further studies demonstrate that displays of parental warmth have a positive relationship with adolescents' saving behaviors. It turns out that the more parents show affection toward their children, the more sense of security and trust is fostered, which then leads teenagers to behave more responsibly with money. In the study "Family processes and adolescents' financial behaviors," the authors found that children were more likely to save for future education and donate to charity if their parents communicated financial values to them.[105] Further evidence asserts that when parents monitored how their adolescent children used money (such as keeping a watchful eye on a teen's bank account), the youths were more likely to own financial assets and exhibit positive attitudes toward personal finance as young adults.[106]

Be grateful if you were raised in a house where money wasn't a source of angst, but instead was used as a tool to instill wholesome financial principles. As it turns out, college students who recall arguments about money during childhood are more likely to carry higher credit card debt, according to a 2007 study.[107] What's more, research done in 2010 highlighted that a lack of parental money arguments, or generally better parental financial communication, is associated with lower financial and psychological stress and higher well-being among college students after controlling for parental socioeconomic status.[108]

Who we are today as savers and investors is undeniably influenced by our upbringing and early experiences. "Disordered Money Behaviors: Development of the Klontz Money Behavior Inventory" identified eight financial detailers that have the potential to sabotage financial wellness, including compulsive buying, pathological gambling, workaholism, financial enabling, financial dependence, and financial denial. The research found that often these debilitating behaviors were based on enmeshment between parents and children.[109]

Financial advisors reading this may be reminded of Klontz Money Scripts. For those unfamiliar, money scripts are our unconscious beliefs and attitudes about money, often formed in childhood and influenced by societal and cultural factors (as evidenced above). Money scripts serve as the foundation for how we perceive, interact with, and make financial decisions throughout life. The underpinning of Klontz's work is that we should strive to be humble enough to recognize that while we are wired a certain way, we can take steps to challenge and transform our beliefs, fostering a healthier and more empowering relationship with money.

Our interaction with financial issues as taught to us (or, more aptly, just absorbed by us through osmosis) reminds me of David

Foster Wallace's speech, "This is Water." Originally a college commencement address, Foster Wallace uses an anecdote about fish to illustrate how often it is that unnoticed factors influence our everyday lives and most deeply held beliefs—including those that are money-related.

The story involves two young fish happily swimming in the ocean who are asked by an older fish, "How's the water?" One of the young fishes turns to the other and asks, "What the hell is water?" Indeed, we can be so immersed in our environment that we fail to recognize and understand what shapes our attitudes and behaviors.

We are all like the young fish in Foster Wallace's analogy, swimming in our money scripts, soaking wet and completely unaware of what water is.

So how do we begin critically examining and, in some cases, working to unlearn the money lessons we've been shown and taught?

To begin, we need a mental scaffolding with which to think about money. Otherwise, it's too ethereal. My own research has found that money values tend to line up along five dimensions:

1. **Communication**: Are you direct or indirect in how you talk about money?
2. **Worry**: Do you worry about your finances a little or a lot?
3. **Function**: Is the purpose of wealth to enjoy today or secure tomorrow?
4. **Orientation**: Is money for individual or collective use?
5. **Importance**: Is money important or unimportant in your vision of the good life?

To begin to understand your money story, imagine each of these as a continuum and try to plot yourself along that spectrum. Next, mark another point to represent the messages you received from your parents or culture about the appropriate place you should exist along each of these five continua. Is there a difference? Finally, make a final dot to plot where you'd like to be.

Carl Jung famously said, "Until you make the unconscious conscious it will direct your life and you will call it fate." For so many of us, we are living out money stories that we inherited and unthinkingly digested as simply "the way it is." There are no good or bad money attitudes in isolation. After all, each of the five approaches above has pros and cons. But there are money stories that are maladaptive for the place and time in which we find ourselves.

Consider the soldier in a war zone who instinctively drops to the floor upon hearing a loud noise: that's adaptive. Now think of that same soldier hitting the deck each time a car backfires in his suburban neighborhood post-deployment. The same behavior, but one approach is adaptive and the other maladaptive based on the reality at hand.

Your money reality was shaped by people and places that were themselves shaped by realities that may or may not look like anything you are experiencing today. It is only by picking up the various pieces of your money life, examining each one closely, and deciding what to keep and discard, that you will be able to write a money story that fits you and the life you want to live.

THE TIME WILL
NEVER BE RIGHT

"**X**EROX THIS FOR me, will ya?"
    Want to totally lose your rapport with the younger crowd at the office? Go ahead and use that phrase when requesting a trip to the copy machine. The once-innovative technology company still holds a special nostalgic place in the hearts of the 50 and up group in corporate America, but 'Xerox' is no longer a verb.

Back in the 1970s work culture, Xerox was among the most pioneering tech outfits around. It revolutionized the way modern offices at that time operated, through its leading copiers and printers. The Palo Alto Research Center (PARC), where Xerox originated, also developed other groundbreaking inventions such as the graphical user interface (GUI), the mouse, and the Ethernet.

In that bygone era, Xerox had the chance to pounce on its cutting-edge product suite and thought leadership by becoming a dominant player in the personal computer market. Its management team recognized that, too. But instead of taking a chance investing in computer research, Xerox management chose to stick with the tried and true, focusing on their core businesses. Along the lines of "nobody goes broke taking a profit," who could have waved a stern finger at Xerox for continuing to rake in cash flow from copy machines—an established and thriving industry?

Where Xerox passed, young entrepreneurs such as Steve Jobs and Bill Gates seized the opportunity. Before long, Apple and Microsoft, among others, would duke it out and become the next generation's tech giants. In a half-baked attempt to grab market share, the Xerox Star hit the market in 1981, but it was too late. The Macintosh and IBM's PC had already established a commanding presence.

Xerox simply waited too long for the right time to show up. The truth is, there probably was never that magic ideal moment. There was going to be risk either way: Jump in too early without a well-constructed plan, and new endeavors could flop in short order; but stand on the sidelines (as Xerox did), and the fast-moving market wouldn't allow latecomers to find a foothold.

I see investors do the same thing all the time.

In many instances, when someone receives a substantial cash windfall, say an inheritance, there's a natural apprehension about investing it right away. The fear of loss can paralyze even the most behaviorally aware people. There is a mix of excitement and nervousness when considering the right time to put that cash to work, and remaining out of the market often feels safest when volatility hits, or after stocks have already rallied.

This is when the value of a financial advisor is truly displayed. That unbiased, experienced perspective helps people acknowledge their instinct to wait for the exact optimal moment to hit the 'buy' button, while simultaneously getting them to act for their own good.

The truth is, there's always something to fear in markets. There is always a new reason to sell it all and stay in cash, or to avoid putting new cash to work.

Consider that since 2007, there have been significant declines in U.S. stocks for a multitude of reasons—and those reasons are rarely known in advance. I mean, did any macro strategists have 'once-in-a-century global pandemic' on their 2020 market-crash bingo cards in Q4 2019? Even if you did predict that a worldwide health crisis was on the agenda, chances are you would have been caught flat-footed during the lockdowns of March 2020 when stocks bottomed.

As the table demonstrates, not a year goes by without something to worry about that feels very legitimate in the moment.

Year	Max Stock Market Decline	Supposed Reason
2007–2009	−57%	Global Financial Crisis
2010	−16%	European Debt Crisis
2011	−19%	Eurozone Crisis
2012	−10%	U.S. Fiscal Cliff
2013	−6%	Taper Tantrum
2014–2016	−15%	Global Slowdown, Political Jitters
2017	−3%	Geopolitical Tensions
2018	−20%	Trade War and Interest Rate Hikes
2019	−7%	Trade War and Global Growth Concerns
2020	−34%	Covid-19 Pandemic and Economic Shutdowns
2021	−5%	Supply Chain Problems
2022	−25%	Inflation, Fed Rate Hikes
2023	−8%	U.S. Regional Banking Turmoil

Whether we're talking business strategy or investing your nest egg, the time will never feel just right to take a risk. The solution is simple for you and me and our money: Have a plan and work with a pro who will make you stick to it.

Let's get back to that hypothetical inheritance mentioned before and put some numbers to it.

Suppose you're 30 years old and inherit $100,000. Nervous about the worry of the day reported by the financial media, you hold off, with the intention to 'buy the dip' when the market drops. The dip never comes. It turns out that it's a year like 2013 or 2017 in which there are no material drops in the stock market. So you wait. And wait. The pain of missing out is gut-wrenching, and you finally capitulate and buy when you hit age 40. The 'all-clear' moment never arrived.

By the time you retire (we'll go with age 65), the investment account is worth $920,378, if we assume you earned 3% in cash for a decade and then 8% annually in the market from age 40 to 65.

Now, had you invested right away, all-in, at age 30, the account balance would be a tidy $1,478,534, assuming 8% growth annually.

That is more than half a million dollars of opportunity cost, all due to standing pat waiting for the right time (which of course never materialized).

Another way to assess the cost is with your time and retirement age. The more modest portfolio would likely result in you needing to work for an additional several years, because you stayed out of the market.

As the graph shows, waiting for the 'all-clear', can be costly in dollars and cents as well as the impact it may have on our personal and professional lives.

Don't wait for the all-clear – portfolio growth of $100,000 from age 30

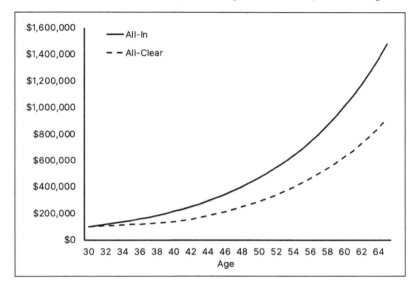

What drives a company like Xerox to avoid taking a strategic risk, and investors like you and me from getting invested in the market as soon as possible?

It's actually not as much waiting for the right time as it is our desire to be perfect. Procrastination is often viewed as a form of laziness, but it is far more often a hallmark of perfectionism. This reality is grounded in our evolutionary preference for safety rather than bliss—we would rather be 'not unhappy' as opposed to 'joyful' if getting to a joyous state requires some risk-taking.

The problem perfectionists encounter time and again is that they set such ambitious standards that they never embark on a risky activity—like Xerox execs needing to dive headlong into the PC market, or Joe Investor facing the decision and action of buying an index fund. Getting caught in a holding pattern due to fear is the result.

Our decision-making processes that matured eons ago on the savannahs of Africa resulted in the prioritization of physical safety, but in today's world, where basic needs are often already met, we're left grappling with different, more internal, issues. This mismatch leads people (including you—you're not that special) to cling to risk-averse tendencies, preventing us from taking the very risks today that could bring us future security and freedom.

There's good news here, though.

The freeing part of there being no real *good* time to invest is, logically, that there's also no *bad* time to invest either. The coast will never be clear and there will never be certainty in markets. Fundamentally, investing is purely a bet on the future being better than today, a reality that humankind has a long history of realizing.

Maybe you're still nervous. Try this: Just start small.

Use behavioral quirks to your advantage by keeping things simple (go with a single diversified fund), automate (through periodic contributions to your 401k, IRA, or taxable brokerage account investments), and educate yourself about the power of long-term investing.

"I'LL BE HAPPY WHEN..." IS A TRAP

TRY SOMETHING FOR me.

I want you to answer the question, "How much money would I need to feel financially secure?" Read on when you've arrived at a specific number in your head.

If you're like most people, the answer to this question is going to be, "A little bit more than I have right now."

But this is a trap.

The truth is 'more' is rarely enough.

This innate feeling of lack so many of us battle with goes back ages.

At very least, we can trace it to the 6th century BCE, where King Croesus of Lydia awaited his execution after being lured by the siren song of power and additional wealth. How he arrived at the funeral pyre is a story that aggressive investors and businesspeople might empathize with, though it's a little more dramatic than most of our lives.

Croesus had ruled over Lydia and was considered among the richest kings of his time. Everything seemed to be going well in his flourishing kingdom and he lived a life of luxury. But he didn't enjoy that opulence. In his search for happiness, he sought the guidance of the Oracle of Delphi, revered for her wisdom and foresight. The Oracle told Croesus that if he waged war against mighty Persia, a great empire would be destroyed. The king took that as a sign to launch a military endeavor against the powerful Persian Empire.

The Oracle's insight proved correct—but it was the great empire of Lydia that was destroyed in the war against Persia.

Croesus had acquired more wealth than most men could dream of, yet he found only dissatisfaction because he always wanted more. He was beholden to an inner thirst that could never be quenched.

You see, Croesus quickly adapted to new wealth, experiencing only a fleeting high from a conquest or lucrative trade deal. This is a behavioral feature with which we are all plagued—the story of Croesus is a prime example of *hedonic adaptation*.

———————————

Successes at work, in relationships, and with money provide us with a temporary psychological boost, but we just as quickly come right back down to reality. The same goes for failures and misfortunes—after a decline, our psyche returns to a baseline level of happiness after a short period of time.

Although this causes some problems in our pursuit of wealth and happiness, it also serves humankind well. Collectively, society is always forging ahead due to an instinctive desire for a better life. The deeply ingrained "not quite there" mentality of humankind has led us to explore oceans, tame the elements, and explore outer space. Hedonic adaptation also helps us assimilate to new environments, and recover from tragedy and grief.

Most important to our daily functioning, hedonic adaptation also gives our brains a break. The process of speedily reverting to a mental equilibrium aids us in coping with the highs and lows of everyday life. Moreover, this psychological phenomenon is like an expert chief financial officer, allocating our brain's resources efficiently. Our cognitive abilities are constantly being shifted to what's needed most for survival and to pounce on new opportunities.

Personal finance gurus often refer to the *hedonic treadmill* to describe the never-ending pursuit of wealth and serenity. But, as money wizard Frank Costanza proved to America, "serenity now" may lead to "insanity later."

So, while the hedonic adaptation helps us in a broad sense and over the long haul, in the short term it can make us do dumb things with our money. Once we become aware of this tendency toward constant seeking and dissatisfaction, the logical next question becomes, "What do I do about it?"

To answer that, here are five practices to help you step off the hedonic treadmill and catch your breath.

GRATITUDE PRACTICE

One of the easiest tactics to recognize how lucky you are is to dedicate a slot on your calendar to practice gratitude. Focusing on and appreciating the good parts of your life can be done through keeping a daily gratitude journal, expressing appreciation for others, and simply saying and giving thanks.

Research conducted by Robert Emmons from the University of California, Davis and Michael McCollough of the University of Miami concluded that consciously focusing on one's blessings may have both material and interpersonal benefits, leading to higher levels of well-being and overall life satisfaction.[110]

MINDFULNESS AND SAVORING

Along with always appreciating what you have, just savoring the present may help overcome hedonic adaptation by increasing awareness of the little things in life. Common activities to achieve this state include meditation, deep breathing exercises, or just taking in a beautiful sunset.

A 2007 study by Bryant and Veroff found that basking in positive experiences can boost overall well-being.[III] We should also heed the sage wisdom of the 1980s American philosopher Ferris Bueller: Life moves pretty fast. If you don't stop and look around once in a while, you could miss it.

INFREQUENT SPLURGES

Perhaps the simplest and most fun method to ditch the hedonic treadmill is to indulge. Who wouldn't want to do that? The trick is to intentionally disrupt your routines and tweak your behaviors.

Here's what I mean: Let's say you usually have a sweet treat after dinner each night. Try making that small activity special by limiting it to just, say, a Saturday night indulgence. Research suggests that you'll enjoy the splurge more and feel healthier in the process. Or let's say you usually budget $200 per month for new clothes. Instead, save up for three months and buy a higher-quality item for $500. The result is both a financial saving and an increase in the felt power of the reward.

VARIETY AND NOVELTY

By allowing yourself to recognize and enjoy special occasions in fresh ways, you bring out those events' uniqueness and pleasures.

For instance, instead of going to the same nice restaurant with a reliably tasty medium-rare filet to celebrate an anniversary, give a new hot spot a shot. Worst-case scenario, you tried something boldly unfamiliar and now have a different story to tell.

Novelty can come in mundane tasks, too. Just taking a new route to work or delving into a new book genre can disrupt hedonic adaptation in your day-to-day life.

EMPHASIZING PEOPLE OVER THINGS

It's no surprise that investing in social connections over material possessions creates long-term happiness. A study conducted in Germany followed nearly 1,200 people over one year. Participants who wrote down at least one social strategy were found to follow through with actions that led to more social engagement, and that group reported increased life satisfaction.[112]

The upshot is that you can better your contentment level by focusing on building relationships with people and putting less emphasis on yourself, and especially some shiny bauble.

How can you go about that? Devote time to having deep conversations with friends and family members, take part in social clubs, or volunteer at an organization near to your heart. All of these social engagements are ways to overcome the negative effects of hedonic adaptation.

Evolutionary and psychological factors wire us to believe that happiness lies right around the corner. It is like a never-ending chase. We become mentally moored to the notion that just by landing one more promotion at work, seeing an extra zero on our net-worth statement, acquiring a luxury car that one-ups the neighbors, or meeting that one special person, then we will reach a Zen level of contentment.

Given that you have incredible taste in literature and are reading a book on finance for fun, you will probably reach one of those goals. But not long after hitting the milestone, though, you will be right back on the hedonic treadmill—longing for happiness once again.

While this never-ending quest for peace may have kept our ancient ancestors hustling for food, its primary function in modern life is to keep us wishing away our todays in search of a brighter tomorrow. And when the longed-for tomorrow arrives, it only amounts to what *Wall Street Journal* writer Jason Zweig refers to as a "neurological yawn."

The antidote to this is a radical focus on the now, deep savoring of all that life brings us, a willingness to experience new things, and a prioritization of people over things. By cultivating this mindset and by taking action, we can counteract the perpetual search for elusive future happiness and find fulfillment in the here and now.

LEARN WHAT
TO IGNORE

L ET YOUR MIND venture back to the time before the iPhone. Hard to do, isn't it? The king of the mobile phone market was BlackBerry, which was especially popular with business users. But the cell phone market overall was highly fragmented. There were so many styles with different user interfaces, and no single product line truly captivated the masses.

Enter Steve Jobs. Visionary that he was, he took a different approach. Jobs recognized that the cell phone market lacked a truly loved device because people were inundated with a flood of new gadgets and platforms that could never reach broad-adoption status. Jobs' single great insight was that mobile phones were just too complicated. From design to interface to software, Jobs knew that he had to cut out the noise and bring people what they didn't even know they wanted.

Jobs and Apple—just a $30 billion market cap company at the time—embarked on a bold mission to craft a device that seamlessly combined phone, internet communications, and music capabilities; the ultimate in simple sophistication. The goal wasn't to bring yet another contraption to the market or to wow anyone with technical prowess for its own sake, but to revolutionize the industry by cutting through the clutter.

Eventually, the iPhone was launched in the summer of 2007. The elegantly simple touch-screen smartphone and user-friendly interface were awe-inspiring to techies and technophobes alike. Its resounding success through simplicity and minimalist design validated the company's approach of aiming for widespread consumer appeal. By late 2007, a new smartphone standard had been set, paving the way for Apple's ascent to become the world's most valuable brand.

Oh, and as for BlackBerry—its management team, fully attuned to the market noise, elected to double down on their spending to improve the phone's keyboard feature.

Yeah, that didn't go well.

Steve Jobs is hardly alone among the accomplished and noteworthy who excelled by harnessing the power of learning to ignore noise. Indeed, it is a common trait of great thinkers and investors throughout the ages. Bestselling author Morgan Housel cites several examples in his piece, "Paying Attention":

Sherlock Holmes says in the book, *The Study of Scarlet*:

I consider that a man's brain originally is like a little empty attic, and you have to stock it with such furniture as you choose. A fool takes in all the lumber of every sort that he comes across, so that the knowledge which might be useful to him gets crowded out, or at best is jumbled up with a lot of other things so that he has a difficulty in laying his hands.

Says Housel, "Francis Crick, who discovered the double helix structure of DNA, was once asked what it takes to win the Nobel

Prize. He responded: 'Oh it's very simple. My secret had been I know what to ignore.'"

And author John Barry writes: "Einstein reportedly once said that his major scientific talent was his ability to look at an enormous number of experiments and journal articles, select the very few that were both correct and important, ignore the rest, and build a theory on the right ones."

This cadre of exceptional thinkers is bound together less by their ability to analyze every piece of data, and more by their ability to see what didn't matter at all. And when it comes to our financial lives, the amount of information that doesn't matter far exceeds the information that does.

The Wall Street Industrial complex gives off the air of importance, with its marble edifices, highly compensated experts, and 24/7 cable news shout fests. But a look under the hood shows that much of what passes for white-shoe research is little more than noise.

In *The Laws of Wealth*, I cited evidence buttressing the argument that financial outlooks are worth less than the paper on which they are printed. Let's review that again now.

Contrarian investor David Dreman found that most (59%) Wall Street 'consensus' forecasts miss their targets by gaps so large as to make the results unusable. These CFA pros either under or overshoot the actual number by more than 15%.[113] Dreman dug deeper and found that from 1973 to 1993, the nearly 80,000 estimates he reviewed had a mere 1-in-170 chance of being within 5% of the actual number.[114] We can glean two conclusions: (1) Forecasting is hard; and (2) Wall Street experts make a lot of noise.

Economist and author James Montier sheds light on the difficulty of forecasting in his *Little Book of Behavioral Investing*. In 2000, the average target price of stocks was 37% above the market price—prices ended up higher by just 16%. In 2008, the average forecast was a 28% increase—the market would go on to decline by 40%. More broadly, a study conducted by Michael Sandretto of Harvard and Sudhir Milkrishnamurthi of MIT analyzed one-year forecasts for the 1,000 most widely covered companies by analysts. They found that the analysts were consistently inconsistent, missing the mark by an annual rate of 31.3% on average.[115]

And how about this: The 2020 consensus return estimate for the S&P 500 was about 3%—the actual gain was 16%, with a 34% crash tossed in partway through the year.[116] What's even more hilarious to consider is how much worse the estimates would have been had the forecasters known that we would endure a global pandemic that year that would shut down the economies of the world. The research is unequivocal—forecasts don't work and, as a corollary, neither do the investment schemes that rely on them.

———————

We now understand that everyone from fictional detectives to wild-haired geniuses benefits from learning to know what to attend to and what to let pass by. Still, even with that understanding, it remains difficult to decipher meaningful signal from noise, especially when the noise arrives in so tidy a package with a compelling story tied to it.

Here are a few mental models to gain clarity from the chaos.

ASK YOURSELF, "DO I HAVE REASON TO BELIEVE THE ACCURACY OF THIS INFORMATION?"

As you read above, if the information in question is an analyst estimate, a financial forecast, or a speculation on a political move, the answer is almost certainly, "No."

ASK YOURSELF, "WHAT IS THE MOTIVATION OF THE PERSON GIVING THE FORECAST?"

It's also worth considering the motivation behind the forecast. Is the person giving it selling a course, promoting a product, or part of a media machine that benefits from rumors of bad news? Humans are naturally self-motivated and a forecast tends to say more about how someone is compensated than what they actually believe will happen in the future.

ASK YOURSELF, "WILL I CARE ABOUT THIS IN FIVE YEARS?"

Go look up a newspaper from five years ago and flip (digitally, I'd guess) to the Politics or Business section. Is that politician's scandal still on your mind today? What about the bad quarter from that large-cap tech darling? I rest my case.

ASK YOURSELF, "DOES THIS MATTER FOR MY FINANCES OR MY SOUL?"

A natural disaster. A war in Europe. A killer virus. Each of these can and should move us to empathize with and mobilize on behalf of those affected. But all too often, the unease we feel from constantly consuming news can generalize to our financial decisions. Not everything that moves you as a human should cause you to move your money.

TIME IS THE
ULTIMATE PURCHASE

Hᴀᴠᴇ ʏᴏᴜ ꜱᴇᴇɴ the film *Freaky Friday*? As the father of a teenage daughter, I can tell you that I have. For the benefit of those who aren't lucky enough to have seen this cinematic masterpiece, let me offer up a quick spoiler. (We'll get to the money stuff in a minute.)

The original movie was released in 1976, with a 2003 remake starring Jamie Lee Curtis and Lindsay Lohan. The original storyline centers around a mom, Ellen, and her daughter, Annabel, mysteriously switching bodies; hilarity and light-hearted conflicts ensue. Early in the movie, we witness the typical clashes between a stressed-out, busy American mother and her testy teenage daughter. However, one morning, they both wake up in shock, realizing that they have switched bodies.

Being in the other's shoes creates challenges—what was once second nature for one turns into seemingly insurmountable tasks for the other. Ellen is forced to handle the drama of high school while Annabel is thrust into taking on adult responsibilities, including her mother's engagement.

After some getting used to the uneasy waters, the two eventually get more comfortable and gain a deeper understanding of the other's daily struggles, fostering a newly found appreciation of their relationship. They solve problems for each other, and values such as communication, understanding, and mutual respect are reinforced within the family.

The body swap resulted in a grown woman and a teenager seeing life from the other's point of view. As a psychologist, the premise provides an interesting behavioral experiment, that I imagine would lead us to deepened levels of empathy and mutual appreciation.

Now that you're familiar with the premise, let me ask you: Would you be willing to embark on a *Freaky Friday*–style life swap with a mystery person described below?

This person is the fifth richest in the world, with a current net worth of $117 billion. This person is well-known throughout the world and widely respected for their intelligence and wit. This person so enjoys what they do that they describe "skipping to work" each day.

Pretty nice setup, right? Are you ready to change places?! What if I told you that this person is also 93 years old and has the self-described dietary habits of a first grader, subsisting primarily on Coke and McDonald's?

By now you've probably guessed that I'm speaking of Warren Buffett. While the initial descriptors of Buffett, such as wealth, happiness, and respect, may have caught your attention, I imagine that you became less interested when I told you about his age.

Why is that?

Because you have an inherent sense that no amount of money is worth what is likely to be a fleeting amount of time left here on Earth. In so doing, you have valued your own remaining time at well over one billion dollars per year! It's not surprising then that so much of the research on how money can improve our lives has to do with buying time.

Time is so much of a valuable commodity that a 2009 study by Tim Kasser and Kennon Sheldon found that having more free time is associated with greater life happiness and satisfaction, even after controlling for income and even among those who say they enjoy being busy. The paper goes on to describe "time affluence," a twist on measuring employee morale—the more daily flexibility workers possess, the more they can feel like the Oracle of Omaha, skipping along to the office each morning.[117]

Of course, salary is important too. In the aptly titled "Valuing time over money is associated with greater happiness," Weidman, Dunn, and Whillans investigated how people value the two most scarce resources: time and money. Their findings revealed that individuals who prioritize time tend to experience higher levels of happiness, even after accounting for materialism and a host of demographic variables.[118] So, next time you are shooting for that promotion at work, be mindful of what it might mean for your often-undervalued spare capacity on the clock.

These pieces of evidence lead us to ponder whether it is worth it to use one scarce resource (money) to buy the scarcest of resources (time). The data suggest it's an increasingly valuable exchange. Consider that incomes around the world are on the rise, yet, according to a 2017 study, individuals with higher salaries are often the most pressed for time. Time scarcity has been linked to lower well-being, including reduced happiness, increased anxiety, and insomnia. A lack of available hours also contributes to unhealthy lifestyle habits, such as neglecting exercise and experiencing higher rates of obesity.

Isn't it ironic that more money should allow us the freedom to outsource annoying tasks, live closer to work, and prioritize a little me-time? Still, this "time famine," as the researchers labeled it, grows worse each passing year.

Underscoring the disconnect between *more money, less time*, it was found that individuals willingly choose not to purchase time when they have the means. While those who bought themselves more hours enjoyed higher levels of overall wellness and lower levels of stress, only about half of the 818 millionaires surveyed spent anything on outsourcing disliked tasks or buying back any of their time.

The authors investigated further by asking 98 working adults how they would spend a $40 windfall. Just 2% of the sample reported that they would make a time-saving purchase.[119]

———————

A growing body of research all points in the same direction: Greater time, not money, should be our pursuit. Moreover, as we are able, we should deploy money to reclaim our time. Easier said than done, and you might feel trepidation at the thought of giving up control.

With this in mind, here are some practical ways to implement the concept:

- **Know the value of your time**: If you make $100,000 per year, that's $1,923 per week, roughly $400 per working day, and call it $50 per hour. Try halving that number to estimate the worth of your leisure time. Is it a good deal to pay someone $25 per hour (or perhaps a bit more) for lawn care, house cleaning, or even your laundry? Probably so.

- **Get closer to work and play**: Research conducted in England found that an additional 20 minutes of commuting per day has a negative impact equivalent to taking a 19% pay cut at work. Considering the average daily commute in America is 50 minutes, you can effectively experience a salary boost by cutting down on time stuck in traffic each Monday through Friday.[120]

- **Leverage technology**: Invest in tools that can automate or streamline workflows. If you are a business owner, don't skimp on the things you use each day. Focus on efficiency and try to avoid the negative aspects of tech, which could result in wasted time.
- **Delegate tasks you hate**: Not all chores or responsibilities need to be outsourced if you genuinely enjoy them. For instance, I love cooking and find it meditative. It's also a perfect time to connect with and work alongside my kids. Mowing the yard, on the other hand, is something I dread. Outsourcing tasks you loathe has the double benefit of repurchasing time and getting out of something you hate.

Buying time is one of the most powerful, yet most overlooked, sources of joy. The problem of using money to get back a few hours in our week just does not seem as *real* as acquiring shiny objects. Evidence suggests, however, that it's a much more reliable path to increasing happiness and reducing stress. Time is truly the one thing that you can buy now that will always be more valuable tomorrow.

WILLPOWER IS OVERRATED

IN 1911, ROALD Amundsen and his small team of expert explorers embarked on a daring mission to become the first to reach the South Pole. Despite being less equipped than a larger team led by Captain Robert Falcon Scott, Amundsen and his crew achieved the extraordinary feat and returned home safely.

How was it that this seemingly less prepared group of men succeeded?

It would be natural to attribute their success to some lofty human trait like strength of will or determination. But the less sexy truth is that having well-structured processes in place to minimize risks and adjust to uncertainty was the real difference between success and failure, life and death.

Ahead of the journey, Amundsen meticulously planned the dangerous mission based on his experiences in the Arctic and Inuit survival techniques he had honed, along with studying polar conditions. In contrast, Scott's Terra Nova Expedition lacked such a strategic approach and experience. Additionally, Amundsen assembled a squad based on skills and expertise, while Scott's group consisted mainly of friends and acquaintances.

Sled dogs also played a pivotal role in Amundsen's group, enabling faster travel across treacherous terrain due to their adaptability to harsh Antarctic conditions. Amundsen did his homework, too—he even studied different breeds before selecting the right breed to help his crew achieve their goal. Conversely, Scott relied on ponies for travel, which while arguably more majestic, were ill-suited for extremely cold temperatures.

One defining trait of history's greatest explorers and pioneers is their ability to assess situations and make necessary changes. At crucial moments, Amundsen would position himself at the rear of the sled team to assess performance and address problems without slowing the group down. He also remained open to altering course and even his mindset: Upon hearing the news that the British were about to embark on a South Pole mission of their own, he went from scientist to competitor. That focus allowed him to reach the destination with fewer distractions.

Still, he remained calculated about efficiency and conserving resources. Amundsen determined in advance how much food and fuel was needed each day and even went to the lengths of organizing supply chain depots along the journey, leaving no vital aspect to chance.[121] Scott, meanwhile, struggled with resource management, which led to severe shortages during his team's journey back home.

The tale of the tape: Amundsen's preparations, processes, adaptability, execution, and risk management led him and his squad to reach the South Pole on December 14, 1911, and return safely. Scott and his group, just as ardent, also made it to the South Pole, more than a month later, on January 17, 1912. They discovered that Amundsen had beaten them to the punch. Scott's team of five perished on their return journey due to harsh conditions, exhaustion, and dwindling supplies.

Both men worked hard and wanted success with every fiber of their being, but only one had the right systems in place. Likewise, there is very little that differentiates one of us from another when it comes to our financial lives. We all want the same thing when it comes to our wealth—abundance—but very few of us put the right structures in place. Instead, we rely on trying to do the right thing. The problem is that willpower only gets us so far.

Author James Clear, known for his bestseller *Atomic Habits*, emphasizes a crucial truth: "You do not rise to the level of your goals, you fall to the level of your systems."

That's seen very sharply when it comes to how we handle our finances. While our goals in other areas of life may vary, our aspirations for money tend to be pretty much the same: We want more of it and we hope it brings us happiness.

If our goals are so uniform, why are our outcomes so divergent?

It is a multi-faceted answer, of course, but a great deal of it has to do with the fact that when it comes to money, wanting and willing an outcome has far less to do with achieving it than we'd like to believe. We need systems in place.

It's not that willpower is unimportant. In fact, self-control is a great trait to possess. A 2012 meta-analysis with more than 32,000 participants found that people who rate themselves high on self-control were happier, did better in school, had better relationships, and were more fit.[122] Being more content and having washboard abs is great, but the problem is that willpower isn't all that dependable.

So, what can we do about that?

To increase the chance that our willpower sticks, behavioral science offers two key approaches: (1) Improve systems to minimize the need for self-control; and (2) change the way that we conceptualize willpower.

A 2011 study tracked 205 people in Germany for a week. They were armed with BlackBerry beepers (yes, it's a bit dated) that would randomly ask them questions about desire, temptation, and self-control. The aim was to explore the frequency, intensity, and conflicts of desires in everyday life, and how (if at all) the participants exercised self-control to resist urges. The results were striking. People who claim to excel at being masters of their desires reported fewer instances of temptation.[123] Later research backed up those findings. That might lead you to conclude that more willpower leads to better outcomes, but there is something else at play here.

A 2017 study involving over 2,000 participants found that those with high levels of self-control mainly had such willpower because they had great habits. These individuals consistently practiced the behaviors we often wish willpower could help us maintain, such as engaging in daily exercise, adopting healthy eating habits, making time for regular reading, and getting a good night's sleep.[124] People who exhibit strong self-control often lead structured lives that minimize the need for decision-making in the face of temptation. So, it's not being strong-willed that results in better outcomes—but rather possessing a solid set of systems.

Let's get practical.

How can we improve our lives and reduce the chance of failure without turning into robots? In "Beyond Willpower: Strategies for Reducing Failures of Self-Control," the authors outline specific habits and strategies that can help us bypass an overreliance on willpower:

- **Commitment devices**: Robert Cialdini long ago showed that we have a natural inclination to live in alignment with our commitments: If you commit to running with a friend, you are more likely to show up. Solo run? Maybe not. When it comes to your money, one of the biggest advantages of working with a financial advisor is the commitment you make to getting your financial house in order.

- **Temptation bundling**: Pair something you want to do with something you may not enjoy or have been putting off. For instance, you promise to treat yourself to a night out on the town with your significant other, but only once you have worked together to create a will or trust.

- **Temptation elimination**: One of the smartest approaches to avoid testing your willpower is to not put yourself in a risky situation in the first place. Alcoholics shouldn't go to bars. Dieters shouldn't keep cookies in the house. And those attempting to maintain a disciplined approach to long-term investing shouldn't check their portfolio daily.

- **Taking a breather**: Rest and distance promote the ability to exercise restraint. After a break, people are often better at adhering to routines or following procedures, like nurses and handwashing.[125] Money consistently tops the list of stressors for people around the world, so there is no shame in setting aside specific times to discuss financial matters to avoid it becoming a constant concern.

- **Mental contrasting**: What does the future look like if you save 20% of your paycheck each month, invest sensibly, and stay the course? Visualize it in detail and consider what opportunities such actions would afford you. Now imagine that you did none of those things. How much different does tomorrow look now?

The first step in the fight against being weak-willed is to create an environment that doesn't require excessive use of willpower, though no amount of careful engineering can ever obviate the need for self-control altogether. What's more, when we need to use willpower, behavioral science has something to say about how it can best be used and conceptualized.

Traditionally, willpower was seen as a finite resource, akin to a battery that depletes with use. However, newer research challenges that long-held take, suggesting that how we perceive willpower significantly impacts our ability to wield it effectively. It's found that people break down into two groups: those with a *limited* mindset and those with a *non-limited* mindset. The former group's willpower is worn down by the accumulation of temptations and as energy is constantly applied, leading to the feeling of running on empty—you might feel this at the end of a long day at the office. The latter group's willpower is strengthened and becomes more resilient in the face of such temptations and difficulties. With the non-limited mindset, think of Type A leaders and athletes who only seem to become more emboldened when encountering obstacles on their path to success.

One of the more interesting case studies of this concept applies to students assessed to have non-limited mindsets who wasted less time ahead of a big exam, thus earning better grades, compared to their limited-mindset peers. Those same students later exerted self-control in other areas like avoiding fast food restaurants and bypassing an impulsive shopping spree. The limited-mindset students—those who believed their willpower ran on empty after a major test—were more likely to indulge in the aforementioned vices after a grueling exam.[126]

We all have largely similar goals when it comes to our money. We want to enjoy what we earned and build enough wealth over time to live out a happier and less stressful future. How you reach your goals is two-pronged, and it isn't dependent so much on how badly you want to achieve them. Like the intrepid explorers of the South Pole, the success of your journey is determined by the effectiveness of the systems in place and how you think about willpower.

SIMPLICITY SAVES

O FTEN, THE BEST answer to our solutions—be they financial or otherwise—lies not in an advanced model or a weighing of all pieces of evidence, but in the quick and obvious.

What is right there under our noses may be more powerful and meaningful than we realize.

One such story is found in the Old Testament and for me it has come to symbolize what I now call "River Jordan Problems," or complex problems with straightforward answers that go unrecognized precisely because they are so simple.

The parable that gave rise to that moniker is that of Naaman, a wealthy man in his society who was also a commander of one of the armies of the King of Syria. By many accounts, he was a man yielding power who was respected within his community for his military prowess. But there was one (big) problem: Naaman was a leper. In an attempt to rid him of this most painful encumbrance, one of Naaman's servants suggested that he consult with a holy man called Elisha in Samaria, who was reputed to work miracles for those similarly afflicted.

Having little to lose, Naaman took his horse and chariot to the home of Elisha, the holy man, and requested an audience with the prophet. Upon arrival, Naaman expected an elaborate ceremony for his healing. Rather than even coming out himself, though, Elisha sent forth a servant with a simple message for Naaman, "Go and wash in (the River) Jordan seven times, and thy flesh shall come again to thee, and thou shalt be clean."

Now, our powerful protagonist was not happy about this exchange on two counts. First, Elisha didn't even have the common decency to speak with him—talk about an insult, particularly in Biblical times. More egregious still was that he was told to perform a seemingly inane task in what is a not-so-pretty river (go ahead, look up 'River Jordan' and see for yourself how muddy it is). Naaman went on to name three rivers more beautiful and more proximal before storming off in a rage.

Incensed as he was, Naaman's servants dared to approach him to suggest that he follow the simple request of the holy man, saying: "My father, if the prophet had bid thee do some great thing, wouldst thou not have done it? How much rather then, when he saith to thee, 'Wash, and be clean?'" As the story goes, Naaman humbled himself, performed the seemingly simple task, and was cleansed of his disease. Awestruck by the miracle and relieved of his doubts, Naaman returned to Elisha to acknowledge God's healing power and offered Elisha gifts in gratitude.

———————

All it took for Naaman to be healed was following basic instructions with a small dose of faith—not some elaborate plan fraught with complexity and pomp. The story of Naaman leads us to ask:

Are there problems in my portfolio, business, and life that have plain answers that I'm overlooking precisely because they are too simple?

As you ponder, we can look to Nassim Taleb, author of *The Black Swan*, for more evidence of how people are wont to avoid an easy fix. As I detailed in *The Laws of Wealth*, Taleb hilariously relates a story about suitcases that speaks to how we think about innovation and how our best efforts to be creative can be thwarted by our tendency to overcomplicate things. As Taleb points out, the wheel was created over 6,000 years ago (even before Naaman's time), but wheeled luggage is a very recent invention.

For years, harried travelers would drag heavy bags through an airport unaided, doing untold damage to bodies and departure times. When relief initially came, it was in the form of a sort of wheeled exoskeleton contraption to which bags could be lashed or bungee-corded; an improvement to be sure, but still unnecessarily cumbersome. It is only in the last few decades that wheels have actually been placed on the luggage itself, an intuitive approach that only took us 6,000 years to achieve.

Taleb says of this concept, "Both governments and universities have done very, very little for innovation and discovery, precisely because, in addition to their blinding rationalism, they look for the complicated, the lurid, the newsworthy, the narrated, the scientistic, and the grandiose, rarely for the wheel on the suitcase."[127]

Don't you agree with Taleb?

I bet you've seen an invention or idea and thought, "Why didn't I think of that?!" The reason you didn't may have a great deal to do with overlooking the elegant power of simplicity.

———

Humankind put a man in space before we put wheels on a suitcase, and we bring that same misguided preoccupation with complexity to our financial lives.

NDP Bookscan tells us that since 2002, there have been about 500 personal finance books written each year, with that number touching 700 in a busy year. In the U.S. alone, there are 8,763 mutual funds, nearly 4,000 hedge funds (with thousands more internationally domiciled), and multiple, 24/7 cable financial news channels devoted, ostensibly, to helping you master money.[128]

All of this gives the impression that sorting out your financial life is very, very complicated indeed. But suppose it's all just a River Jordan Problem, and that what it takes to be healed of bad financial behavior is a quick dip in a muddy river.

A prime example comes from the world of measuring fund returns. Shows like *Billions* convey to the audience that the drivers of fund performance are high-speed computing, co-location, an army of Ivy League quants, or a Transatlantic fiber optic cable that shaves five milliseconds off processing times (that's a true story, by the way).[129]

But what if I told you that the key determinant of fund returns is shockingly simple and painfully obvious—fees. Morningstar is constantly running the numbers on this, X-raying managed funds from every angle to see what emerging trends could help retail investors and financial advisors alike. The findings are consistent and robust. The total cost you pay for an ETF or mutual fund is the best predictor of future success. It isn't the manager's tenure, the number of CFA charterholders on staff, a hidden code tucked away in a black box, or innate stock-picking intuition that separates mutual fund returns.

In the analysis, U.S. equity funds were sliced into quintiles by net annual expense ratio. It turned out that the lowest-cost batch boasted a total return success rate of 62%, outperforming the second-lowest quintile's 48% rate, followed by 39% for the mid-range funds, 30% for the second-costliest quintile, and 20% for the most expensive group. Morningstar concluded that the cheaper the quintile, the better the returns, all else equal. Overall, funds in the lowest-cost quintile had three times the probability of success compared to those in the priciest quintile.

So, want to keep things simple with your asset allocation? You can ignore the compelling story told by the fund managers and gloss over its chic annual report. Just look at the fund's annual expense ratio relative to its peer group.

Most of us are just like Naaman. We are harried travelers stumbling through the airport with sub-par suitcases.

In the investment space, all too often enthralling narratives and jargon lend the impression that one money manager is better than the rest. It's hard to blame anyone for buying into the complex. In fact, it is that normative response upon which the Wall Street marketing pounces.

But once we understand how much we have in common with stubborn ole Naaman, it becomes more evident that simple truths carry the biggest weight when it comes to optimizing your finances.

To harness the power of financial simplicity in your life, ask yourself the following:

- Am I maximizing my human potential at work?
- Am I automatically saving a meaningful percentage of my income?
- Are those savings diversified within and between asset classes?
- Am I paying a fair fee for the products and advice I'm using?
- Am I seeking out support and guidance in areas where I am not an expert?

If you can answer affirmatively to all these questions, you are ahead of 90% of your peers and, yes, you will even outperform a similar proportion of professional investors.

To paraphrase Einstein, we cannot solve a problem with the same kind of thinking that created it. While it's true that markets are complex, dynamic systems that are constantly evolving, what is equally undeniable is that it is only by countering that complexity with elegant simplicity that we are ever able to be financially free.

WHAT DOESN'T KILL YOU MIGHT MAKE YOU RICHER

NELSON MANDELA'S LIFE story is among the most inspiring human examples of resilience, transformation, and leadership. Trauma and travails shaped the man he evolved to become over the decades. The pain he endured, and his imprisonment, were the crucibles to form his graceful character.

Before becoming South Africa's first Black president, Mandela was a prominent anti-apartheid activist and spent nearly three decades in prison as a result of his bold political stances. Facing isolation, physical labor, and awful living conditions, it would have been easy for him to lose hope in both his political fight and in people writ large.

Mandela took a different approach, however. He leveraged his time in prison to educate himself and engage in political discussions with fellow inmates. Altruism and the constant pursuit of justice grew in his heart. In *Long Walk To Freedom*, Nelson wrote, "I realized that they could take everything from me except my mind and my heart. They could not take those things. Those things I still had control over. And I decided not to give them away."

Those activities and that mindset strengthened his unwavering resolve for justice. He would eventually emerge from prison as a symbol of both resilience and forgiveness. Following his 1990 release, he continued his mission for unity and equality. "I dream of an Africa which is in peace with itself," Mandela said. Upon that philosophical rock, he was driven to play significant roles in leading South Africa's transition to democracy, earning him admiration on the global stage. Then, in 1994, he ascended to become the nation's president, a role he leveraged to bring about a united, non-racial South Africa.

Adversity influenced Mandela's development as a political leader and a man in several ways. The fires of his perseverance and commitment to human rights were stoked during his imprisonment. He witnessed racial segregation, pervasive discriminatory practices, and oppression imposed by the apartheid regime. But he countered humankind's dark side with the shining light of empathy and reconciliation. He also fostered forgiveness rather than continuing a cycle of violence in South Africa, and the empathy he had with people from every walk of life captured adoration internationally. Adversity also influenced his leadership style: 27 years in prison, thoughtfully holding political talks with inmates, honed his strategic thinking prowess and made more salient his vision for a democratic South Africa. Finally, the apartheid's subjugation underscored the importance of inclusivity if his nation were to unite. His empathetic nature to help find common ground was formed through years of politically driven tribulations.

But what made Mandela such a remarkable leader, full of grace, and with an enduring vision for a better world?

Let's turn to a few psychological constructs that help explain it.

I'd like to introduce you to a model that will change your life—

financial or otherwise—if you let it: the ABC model from cognitive behavioral therapy.

Dr. Albert Ellis created this framework to help people challenge irrational thoughts and cognitive distortions. Its name comes from its three components:

- **A. Adversity** or activating event.
- **B.** Your **beliefs** about the event, which encompass both overt and underlying thoughts about situations, yourself, and others.
- **C. Consequences**, which include your behavioral and emotional responses.

We tend to think that our lives are as good or as bad as the things that happen to us, but the ABC model presents a different, and more empowering, vision.

We are not simply trauma sponges being tossed to and fro by the storms of life. The ABC model suggests that how we react to and process the things that happen to us is at least as powerful as the events themselves. As my professional hero, Viktor Frankl, said much more beautifully, "Between stimulus and response there is a space. In that space is our power to choose our response. In our response lies our growth and our freedom."

———

Turning to our finances, *how do you handle trauma in your relationship with money?*

The truth is, financial hardship is extremely widespread, even in some of the wealthiest countries on Earth. The most recent Stress in America study found that 65% of Americans are stressed about money, the highest level in almost a decade.[130] More disturbing, research psychologist Dr. Galen Buckwalter says that 23% of adults and 36% of millennials have experienced financial stress so severe that it could qualify for a diagnosis of PTSD.[131]

To be clear, I am not glorifying suffering, nor am I glad that financial stress and pain are so prevalent. Some hurts, money-related and otherwise, are so deep and so immediate that they must be treated with some combination of professional help and by removing oneself from the pain-inducing stimulus.

I am a doctor of psychology and believe deeply in the power of therapy and professional help. I also believe the words of Frankl: "In some ways, suffering ceases to be suffering at the moment it finds a meaning." Once you identify why you feel trepidation about your finances or a particular money situation, you stand a better chance of recognizing its deeper meaning. That is a necessary step to overcoming adversity—the key to unlocking true personal growth.

Drawing inspiration from Frankl, Mandela, and the ABC model, let's explore the idea of post-traumatic growth (PTG). The concept refers to the psychological changes that can transpire in the wake of a challenging event. These are often good changes—personal growth, heightened resilience, and positive transformations in various aspects of life. While distress and anxiety might spring to mind when mentioning 'trauma', PTG suggests that we can find meaning in those 'I can't handle this' periods.

As exemplified by Mandela, pushing through grim times can lead to development and the unearthing of a deeper purpose amidst life's adversities.

While everyone's experience of PTG may be different, here are some common ways people report progress in the wake of hardship:

- **New possibilities**: Trauma can alter your self-perception and worldview. PTG opens new doors and lets you see different life paths you once never thought you could embark down.

- **Renewed strength**: Mandela boldly took on societal challenges after his persecution. This personal resilience is commonly seen in PTG cases. You may find new ways of coping with difficult situations and realize a greater inner strength to face future adversity.
- **Deeper relationships**: Trauma fosters closer human connections. You've probably felt this during certain stages of life where you realized, "I don't 'got this.'" Leaning on loved ones and appreciating them for being there is the rocket fuel for more meaningful and fulfilling relationships.
- **Spiritual growth**: Humbling adversity causes some people to rethink their deepest beliefs and values. PTG commonly sparks contemplation of life's purpose. Just like Frankl delved into mankind's search for meaning, you will likely experience spiritual maturity.
- **Joie de vivre**: PTG delivers more appreciation for the little things, too. More joy and gratitude, along with a general sense of optimism, increase life satisfaction.

Gentle reader, I hope that your life is one of ease and comfort and that life's richest blessings accompany you always. But if you find, as most of us do, that financial fortune is unkind from time to time, know that hardships can give you experience, new perspectives, and a sense of the depth of your capabilities that might have otherwise remained untapped.

As you think back on your toughest financial times, ask yourself:

- What did I learn from this experience that has improved my money life today?

- What do I know or understand about my own strength for having lived through this?
- How are my priorities better aligned with my 'why' as a result of this hardship?
- Are there ways in which I live with greater urgency as a consequence?

Life is hard; sometimes brutally so. But as Mandela, Frankl, and countless others have shown us, it's during those worst moments (sometimes lasting years or decades) when incredible growth can take place.

Will you go on to lead a great people to freedom or inspire millions to better grasp the meaning of life? Probably not, but you never know.

Surely, though, you can take solace in knowing that even in the midst of suffering and in the heat of the moment, you have the freedom to choose your attitude and find purpose. It is in the furnace of challenges that we are pushed beyond our comfort zones, compelled to confront limitations, and motivated to activate untapped potential.

THE JONESES
AREN'T THAT HAPPY

"**K**EEPING UP WITH the Joneses" has long been a phrase to describe our proclivity to compare ourselves to others. Its origins are not pinned down, but there are a few possible explanations for why it has become a part of American personal finance parlance.

One theory is that "keeping up with the Joneses" came about in the early-20th-century comic strip *Keeping Up with the Joneses*. Makes sense. *The New York Globe's* funny pages ran the cartoon until 1938 and it was picked up in other newspapers. The strip depicted the McGinnis family and their never-ending pursuit to not fall behind their neighbors, the Joneses (who were never seen in the comic).

Another supposition is that "the Joneses" referred to a wealthy New York family who owned a chunk of the former Chemical Bank. The family built impressive villas across the Hudson Valley, well beyond what the typical American dwelling looked like. It stands to reason that the public would view this well-off family with a dash of envy.

Or it might just be that Jones is such a common name, and we probably all know someone with that name. Ergo, there are always people who have more money, a bigger house, and fancier toys than you.

Whatever the root, we can all blame the Joneses for our financial shortcomings. The phrase is a reminder that it's in our flawed nature to compare ourselves to others, particularly people we see and interact with every day. Money insecurity leads us to compete and not appreciate what we have.

Also true, though, is that the research shows one thing for certain: The Joneses aren't very happy.

"Keeping up with the Joneses" is an idiomatic way of talking about materialism, a construct that, it turns out, has three distinctive parts: possessiveness, non-generosity, and envy.[132]

Possessiveness describes our inclination to strive for control of tangible assets, memorable experiences, symbols important to us, and even other people. The lust of the eyes commonly develops when peeking over the fence or, maybe more pervasive these days, scrolling through Instagram and other social media.

Non-generosity fits into the "Keeping up with the Joneses" aura as it underscores our unwillingness to share with others. Just like toddlers fighting over the same plaything when there are dozens more an arm's length away, mimetic behavior often gets the better of us as adults, too. Our ego may produce overall unhappiness and social alienation.

Finally, *envy* might be the worst of the trio. It results in outright displeasure and ill-will towards others' success and perceived happiness. It's common to feel it when we spot designer items in another family's home, or powerful machines in another family's garage. Envy can lead to destructive acts when taken to an extreme, all in an effort to boost one's own self-esteem at the expense of others.

And while materialism looks great from the outside looking

in (who doesn't want a garage full of nice cars?!), the internal experience of materialism is far darker than one might guess.

An examination of 259 different independent samples found that materialism was "associated with significantly lower well-being" and was a poor way of meeting psychological needs. The researchers' findings suggest that this association holds across different demographics, participants, and cultural factors.[133] Another meta-analysis of 92 studies found that those pursuing goals of growth, community, giving, and health experienced significantly higher levels of well-being than those pursuing the Jones-y goals of wealth, fame, or beauty.

The takeaway here is that focusing on intrinsic aspirations related to personal growth, improved relationships, community involvement, and your health stands a better chance of finding lasting joy.[134] Tell that to Mr. and Mrs. Jones at your next cookout.

Your pursuit to keep pace also wears you down mentally. A 1993 research paper authored by Kasser and Ryan found that people placing a high priority on money-related values showed lower psychological well-being compared to those who prioritize more communal and shared goals.[135] There's just nothing good about chasing what isn't ours, and it is not just an American thing. It turns out that Aussies with elevated levels of materialism were "less satisfied with life as a whole," according to a study sampling 162 adults.[136]

So, why is the phenomenon of keeping up with the Joneses so ubiquitous?

A 1998 exploration by M. Joseph Sirgy, a management psychologist, offered insights into the detrimental impact of materialism on well-being. To quote the study:

Materialists experience dissatisfaction with their standard of living because they set standard-of-living goals that are inflated and unrealistically high... Materialists' ideal standard-of-living expectations are influenced by social comparisons involving remote referents... Thus, materialists compare themselves with others that seem to have more income and worked no harder. These equity comparisons generate feelings of inequity, injustice, anger, or envy.[137]

Think about the danger of this approach in the world of social media and limitless streaming content—we are able to compare ourselves to people across the globe who flaunt their wealth and the seeming ease with which it was acquired. In a world where many influencers are famous for being famous, it can feel to the materialist as though everyone is richer than they are and became so through little effort. The truth is that we don't know all that's going on in the lives of our neighbors and celebrities. We all struggle while commonly overlooking our many blessings.

At the same time, it's reasonable to assume that people we know feel just as envious of what *we* possess.

The plight of the Joneses, truly understood, becomes less enviable and more pitiable; the desire to create envy instead of community is a lonely existence.

———

There is hope, though. Here are some evidence-based steps to promote happiness:

1. **Foster better relationships**: Connectedness with loved ones can help promote well-being and reduce the negative effects of materialism. Resolve to spend time with friends and family and reduce social media screentime.
2. **Discover your purpose(s)**: Fulfillment often comes from engaging in activities that inspire us and contributing to causes that ignite our passions. Helping others and making a positive

difference reclaims control over our emotions and actions, breaking free from the influence of materialism.

3. **Practice gratitude**: Being thankful for what you have might be the very first step in bypassing what the Joneses dangle in front of us. Maybe try keeping a gratitude journal or begin your day in humble meditation.

4. **Live for today**: Materialism often stems from a yearning for a better future. However, by shifting our focus to the present, we increase our chances of curbing envious cravings.

5. **Consume less**: Decluttering has its merits. My room full of classic guitars may not align with this principle, but adopting a mindset of acquiring fewer possessions and appreciating simplicity may curtail us from living a materialistic lifestyle.

Our consumer-driven culture and never-ending social media feeds perpetuate materialism and the dubious desire to compare ourselves to others. But you don't have to be a prisoner of possessiveness, a lack of generosity, and nefarious envy. Rather than race to keep up with the Joneses, reach out a helping hand to them, and seek appreciation in your everyday life.

THE POWER OF GRATITUDE

For those of us (like me) who are chronically online, it's easy to take a dim view of interpersonal interactions in the modern world. Social media all too often devolves into unhealthy exchanges that would never occur in the real world and today's trending topic is almost invariably something negative and sensational.

But once we set the phone down, we realize there's actually a lot to like about humanity. We start to notice little things that foster positive sentiment, making each day a bit more enjoyable. We see how something as simple as saying "thank you" can work wonders.

Seasoned readers might recall a movement that grabbed hold across Europe following World War II. The Gratitude Train emerged in the wake of the war's devastation as many nations faced major challenges in rebuilding their communities and their lives. The United States wished to express its solidarity with its allies and neighbors across the pond—the Friendship Train was formed, and it quickly gained a head of steam. Across the nation, thousands of Americans contributed food, clothing, and other essential supplies to be sent to Europe as a symbol of unity and compassion.

The people of France were deeply moved by these random acts of kindness. One French woman, Marthe Richard, devised a campaign to reciprocate this benevolence. Richard led an initiative to collect gifts and donations from the citizens of war-torn France, aiming to stuff an entire train with items and tokens to ship to America out of warm appreciation.

The Gratitude Train, also known as the Merci Train, set forth from France in 1949, toting 49 boxcars brimming with gifts. Each car was adorned with murals and special items, and inside, a treasure trove awaited—including French paintings, sculptures, rare books, and, most precious of all, personal letters of gratitude. Upon arrival in the States, the gifts were distributed among museums, libraries, schools, and other institutions.

The goodwill story of the Gratitude Train serves as a testament to the profound effects that actions of thankfulness can have on individuals, communities, and even among the world's biggest countries. It shows how gratitude can turn a despondent nation into one of hope and pride. Just as a social media star's TikTok can go viral, so too can the best parts of human nature under the right circumstances.

In America today, we are instructed from an early age to say, "thank you," but typically this is more a social nicety rather than something truly transformational, which dramatically undersells the ability of genuine gratitude to impact our lives.

Let's change that in some small way. We can lean into empirical evidence to discover how to go about it.

One powerful method of expressing gratitude is journaling. Taking just five minutes a day to write about what we are grateful for can increase our long-term happiness by over 10%, according to a 2005 study.[138] This research referenced previous work by Dr. Martin E. P. Seligman, a psychologist at the University of Pennsylvania, that tested the impact of several positive psychology interventions on 411 participants.

In the experiment, subjects were instructed to write and hand-deliver a gratitude letter to someone they neglected to thank at one point in their lives or another. After completing the task, Seligman and his colleagues found that there was a massive spike in happiness scores, greater than any other intervention type tested. Perhaps the most remarkable part of the results was that psychological benefits for the letter writer persisted for an entire month.[139]

Journaling and expressing thanks can indeed take our well-being up a few notches. The list of evidence-based benefits is downright gaudy: more positive emotions (Amin, 2014), increased self-esteem (Rash, Matsuba, & Prkachin, 2011), a better love life (Algoe, Fredrickson, & Gable, 2013), deeper friendships (Lambert & Fincham, 2011), decision-making acumen (DeSteno, Li, Dickens, & Lerner, 2014), reduced blood pressure (Shipon, 1977), a lower risk of depression (Seligman et al., 2005), and the list goes on.[140]

But this is a book about money, so can gratitude help us make and keep more dough?

I am grateful that you asked (I'm sorry, I couldn't help myself).

Let's begin on the job and show how you can boost your company's bottom line with one simple behavioral trick.

Among the litany of upsides, it turns out that gratitude is also an incredible leadership hack. A study conducted by researchers at the Wharton School at the University of Pennsylvania found that managers who express gratitude by saying "thank you" to their employees may notice increased motivation and harder work from their staff.

In the study, an experiment was conducted in which university fundraisers were split into two groups. One group made phone calls for donations as usual, while the other group received a pep talk from the director of annual giving, expressing appreciation for their efforts. The results showed that the employees who heard the message of gratitude made 50% more fundraising calls during the following week compared to those who did not receive the message.[141]

There is increasing evidence suggesting that the right mental mindset and an attitude of gratitude can improve performance on the job and in life. A 2015 study tested the effectiveness of an online positive psychology intervention on Greek healthcare professionals who were experiencing depression, anxiety, stress, and burnout. The intervention group, exposed to weekly positive psychology activities, showed significant reductions in depression, anxiety, stress, and emotional exhaustion, along with increased satisfaction with life, compared to the control group.[142]

So, beneficial psychology strategies, including performing acts of gratitude, can have benefits that start at work and stretch into our daily living.

Moreover, gratitude is among six key areas that are shown to enhance the sense of meaning in work, leading to greater effectiveness and fulfillment in one's job. (The others are: strengths finding, positive emotions and flow, work hope, job crafting, and perceiving and living a calling.)[143]

And if you are in the corporate boardroom, humility and thankfulness can help you think big picture. According to 2014 research, people with a higher level of gratitude tend to exhibit less impatience in economic decision-making, resulting in better choices and reduced pressure from seeking short-term gratification.[144]

Of course, this works at the personal finance level, too. After all, the most crucial financial hack of all lies in delaying gratification and pushing back against hyperbolic discounting (aka present bias). As we discuss elsewhere in the book, this ability to resist immediate desires and opt for long-term benefits can significantly impact our financial well-being and lead to better decisions with our money.

A thorough review of the gratitude literature, of which this is just a small taste, leaves us wondering, "Is there any part of life that gratitude can't make better?"

———————

For those seeking practical ways to implement more thankful living, try the following:

- **Gratitude rituals**: Establish routines like saying a prayer before bedtime or reflecting on the best thing that happened during the day at dinner.
- **Giving back**: While talking about what you're thankful for is powerful, engaging in acts of service embodies gratitude in action. Get out there and give back.
- **Gratitude walks**: Take a long, leisurely walk, focusing the entire walk on things you are grateful for and the beauty you see along the way.
- **Thank someone who has been overlooked**: Some of the most profound positive effects in gratitude literature often come from thanking someone whose contributions have been unappreciated or overlooked. Right that wrong today by sending a heartfelt letter.
- **Practice gratitude meditation**: Engage in gratitude meditation, directing your thoughts toward things you are thankful for. This practice has been linked to increased positive emotions and reduced feelings of anxiety and depression.

Among all the self-help tips available in bookstores these days, gratitude has proven to be as close to an elixir as we can find. Thankfulness and appreciation result in better job performance, improved health, and getting your head right when it comes to making the best money decisions.

Adopt some of the strategies noted here. Your future self will surely say, "*Merci.*"

IF YOU CAN'T
SEE IT, YOU WON'T
ACHIEVE IT

W HAT ARE YOUR financial goals? Yes, seriously. What are they?
Take a moment to either write them down or voice
them aloud, ignoring momentarily that you're talking to yourself.

Now, review your list. If you're like most people, it's going to
look something like this:

- Go on a vacation
- Pay off my debt
- Send my kids to college
- Have enough saved up to retire someday

These are all worthy money ambitions, to be sure, but they lack a
critical component that psychologists have shown to be key to goal
achievement: salience.

Before I dive into the particulars of salience, let's learn a lesson on the topic from none other than the most decorated Olympian in history, Michael Phelps.

The GOAT of swimming harnessed the power of salience through visualization. It was by closing his eyes, picturing himself shooting through the water like a torpedo, and then later standing atop the podium as the Star-Spangled Banner played along with the American flag rising toward the rafters, that instilled in his mind that he was going to win gold.

But his mental rehearsal was also meticulous. Before the race, he would be in a Zen-like state, going through each stroke and turn, all the way to the final reach for the wall. He visualized the little things, too, such as the sound of the starting gun to the feel of the cool water against his skin.

If you go back and watch some old footage from any of the 23 gold-medal-winning races he performed, you'll find that he had a routine as he prepared for the race. Preparation, in fact, was a crucial part of the visualization and salience process. Phelps recognized that he could only control what he could do. The Olympian would envision how the race would unfold, but also how it might go right and wrong. That scenario analysis left little room for an energy-draining surprise once he was up on that block.

The process honed his technique and readied himself for any unexpected challenges or setbacks leading up to a meet and during the race. It was through this rigorous mental exercise that he trained his psyche to be confident and focused, maximizing his skills in the water.

I'd say it worked. From 2004 to 2016, he won a total of 28 Olympic medals and currently holds dozens of world records. While not all of his success on the world stage can be attributed to visualization, the technique was undoubtedly part of his competitive edge.

The psychological blueprint that is formed in the mind through visualization helps athletes enhance their performance, build confidence, and overcome mental obstacles that often trip up less prepared competitors.

Visualization is not confined to the pool, though. You too can utilize its power.

With the benefit of Mr. Phelps's example, let's revisit the topic of salience, which is simply how vivid or emotionally striking our visualization of a concept is. We won't go off the deep end here, I promise. Rather, this is a powerful technique to turn vague goals into sharp reality in your brain.

Phelps created stunning visuals, brimming with emotion, and rich in detail, during his pre-game routine. On the other hand, your goal to "have enough saved to retire someday" lacks a certain something. Like a bland meal, we must zhuzh it up.

You see, broad financial goals are the equivalent of Michael Phelps saying, "I'd like to swim across the pool," before starting the 200-meter butterfly. Until we learn to vividly visualize victory, we will be leaving some essential psychological aid on the table.

If this all sounds like feel-good nonsense, I would point you to the research of Dr. Brad Klontz, who found that deep visualization, paired with a process of automating good behavior, can boost personal savings by 73%.[145] Klontz, the creator of Money Scripts that reveal our financial belief patterns, observed that visualization generates a sense of motivation and personal determination, tapping into the power of positive thinking, so to speak. Automation, meanwhile, gives our brains a rest since it doesn't require willpower. Rather, streamlining your finances through today's user-friendly tools makes saving more a breeze.

If you're now bought in and want the power of salience to work on your behalf, I'd offer the following as places to start envisioning a financial future that is truly worth dreaming about:

1. **Mental rehearsal:** Just as Phelps would envision a race's every detail from start to finish, crafting that mental blueprint of what he aimed to achieve, the rehearsal in your mind might begin with waking up on the first morning of retirement with a full slate of activities centered around what's important to you. Picture yourself walking downstairs to make that first cup of coffee, then calling up an old friend for lunch. Imagine planning out regular trips to visit family around the country. Mentally rehearsing your retirement helps to feel that joie de vivre of your golden years.

2. **Sensory imagery:** The swimming GOAT engaged all his senses during his visualization routine. From the gun firing to his body splashing into the pool, even the smell of the chlorine, all to make the endeavor more real in his mind. You can make your money goals vivid in the same way. If you want to retire, then where to? The beach? OK, which beach? What will your beach house look like? What will the sand feel like between your toes? How refreshing is that cool drink in your hand on a warm summer's day? Do you hear the sea breeze landing upon palm fronds? A salient financial goal should viscerally involve all your senses.

3. **Emotional engagement:** Phelps connected emotionally with his mental maps. He tapped into the feelings of confidence, excitement, and fulfillment that he would experience once he stood on that podium in victory. By reaching into his deepest feelings and athletic ambitions through visualization, his mission was emboldened, inspiring him to work harder toward his objectives. For you, it's key to understanding that money is inherently emotional. As I wrote in *The Behavioral Investor*, money has more power to excite than even sex, death, politics, or religion! Likewise, your goals should be emotionally exciting when you share them with an advisor or a loved one. Just as surely as negative emotions like fear can lead us to abandon a

financial plan, salient, positive visualizations can see us through the tough times and help us keep our eye on whatever the prize may be.

―――――――――――

I started by asking you to name a few of your financial goals, and if you're like most people, they were probably a little sterile and, let's be honest, boring.

By engaging each of your senses and devoting time to embracing the power of visualization, you can put psychology on your side, helping you to establish meaningful and specific goals. You'll soon be living out your values and having a little fun in the process.

INVESTING IS AN ACT OF RADICAL OPTIMISM

H
UMANS HAVE A tendency to romantacize the past, a trick of the mind psychologists call 'rosy retrospection'.

As a consequence of our rose-colored lookback, it's easy to imagine that the doom and negativity that pervade modern-day headlines are a recent creation. But communicators of all stripes have long understood that fear sells and therefore convincing narratives of impending disaster are nothing new.

For evidence of this, let's visit the late 18th century. Thomas Robert Malthus is best known for the Malthusian Catastrophe, which postulated that population growth would eventually outstrip the Earth's resources, leading to widespread famine, disease, and the breakdown of society.

The Malthus Prophecy theorized that exponential population growth paired with arithmetically increasing food production was a recipe for disaster that would lead to a crisis of resources including, land, water, and energy. In a snowball effect, humans would quickly see and feel scarcity as deprivation swept across the planet. Malthus predicted that overcrowding, poor sanitation, and a lack of food would result in widespread suffering and pandemics.

To ameliorate this inevitable series of crises, the English cleric proposed two mechanisms to limit population growth.

Here's where it gets disturbing.

First, so-called 'positive checks' to reduce the global population referred to higher mortality rates via increased conflict and malnutrition, as well as more loss of life from natural disasters. These natural checks would couple with 'preventative checks' imposed by humans, such as limits on reproduction, delaying marriage to later in life, and urging people to practice either abstinence or contraception. Unless population growth was throttled, Malthus posited, mass suffering would ensue, and society would collapse.

There has been much debate in the more than 200 years since his *An Essay on the Principle of Population* was published. There's no denying, however, that the world is in a pretty good spot when objectively analyzing key stats. Mr. Malthus would probably be shocked to learn that life expectancy today is more than 70 years old (even after the Covid-19-induced decline). Contrast that to just 28.5 years (33.3 for Europe) in 1800.[146]

Infectious diseases are much less a threat today, too. Smallpox, for instance, had been responsible for killing one-third of those who caught it. A vaccine brought about by innovation and technology had by 1980 nixed it as a major global danger.[147] Maybe the most encouraging trend of all since Malthus's days is child mortality. In 1800, for children under the age of five in the U.S., there were 463 deaths per thousand births. That means for every 1,000 babies born in 1800, more than 46% did not survive to their fifth birthday. Today, that figure is about seven per 1,000.[148]

I'm not saying everything is great everywhere all the time. There are absolutely parts of the world that are not nearly as fortunate as those of us in developed countries. But broad trends suggest that our lives are better now than they were centuries ago.

———————

Malthus is not a one-off in the history of socioeconomics. There have been a host of other Doomsday predictions that have not materialized. Some of them even sound rather convincing if you ask me. Bold, pessimistic predictions spoken with an authoritative tone can be powerful and persuasive. Here are just five examples:

1. *The Population Bomb* (1968) predicted that population proliferation would result in severe food shortages. In that work by Paul Ehrlich, the X-date was purported to be the late 20th century. Swing and a miss. Advancements in agricultural technology and better food production logistics have made that 'bomb' more of a dud.

2. In the 1970s and 1980s, acid rain was said to be the next major risk to humankind. Certainly, industrial activity has some negative impacts on localized ecosystems, but damages have been confined. What's more, regulations and mitigation efforts have greatly reduced acid rain's negative impact.

3. The 1970s and as recently as the mid-2000s featured fears that global oil reserves would be depleted, leading to an energy crisis and severe stress on the economic system, along with social unrest. Technology again came to the rescue through innovative drilling techniques and the ongoing transition to renewable energy development.

4. Yet another Doomsday prediction failed to live up to the hype in the 1990s. The Digital Dark Age where technological obsolescence would render computerized data inaccessible, yielding a loss of essential information and knowledge, had a bright ending at the turn of the millennium. Forward strides in digital preservation of data have mitigated some risks, and cybersecurity is in fact a sprawling industry today, but concerns about privacy remain heightened.

5. My personal favorite: The Mayan Apocalypse of 2012. December 21, 2012, to be precise. Many of us recall how the Mayan Long

Count calendar called for the end of the world on that date. It became a great social media meme. Ultimately, it came and went, with no apocalyptic event. Another one debunked.

In each case, intelligent (and often, well-meaning) individuals and groups set forth a vision for the future so grim that it scared scores of people, catalyzed action, and produced meaningful economic ripples. And each time, it fizzled, giving way to a future that, while not perfect, was hardly as dark as the one imagined.

What is it about our psychology that makes us so susceptible to this sort of fearmongering and what can we do about it?

It turns out that humans have a very real tendency to conflate negativity with intelligence, and that confusion steers our brains to label Doomsday prophets as big-brained-fortune tellers who know what lies around the corner.

I see this play out on social media all the time. You probably do as well. Bombastic and negative tweets, shocking TikToks, and critical blog posts are shown to garner more eyeballs than cheery takes on contemporary mores. There's a term for it: hypercriticism.

Research on this phenomenon dates back to the 1980s, when Teresa Amabile of the Harvard Business School conducted an experiment. She took a group of students and asked them to evaluate two versions of the same book review: one negative, one positive. The group of 55 students thought the negative reviewer was smarter and more competent, also "less warm and more cruel."

This proclivity for negativity is also apparent when we want to sound smart to others. Bryan Gibson, a psychologist at Central Michigan University, asked students to watch a short film, then write a review that each would give to a partner. The twist in this study was that Gibson instructed some of the student-critics to try to make their peer feel warm while others were told to try to appear smart. Those aiming to give the impression of intelligence were viewed as nastier and more bitter.

So, we live in a society where undue credit is given to the most negative among us. Meanwhile, the world keeps spinning into the future, and getting better all the time. People are living longer and healthier lives, are more educated than ever, and poverty has fallen from 80% of the global population in 1800 to under 10% today.[149]

Maybe more salient, U.S. auto fatalities per 100,000 population peaked in 1937 at 29.4. By 2021, it was less than 13. Total motor vehicle deaths hit a high in 1972 at 54,589, but despite millions more drivers on the road, the fatality total dropped by more than 12,000 some 49 years later.[150]

One more for all those in favor of working less—total hours worked annually per individual in the United States in 1870 summed to 3,096, but by 2017, that figure was down 43% to 1,757.[151] Despite modern day's mindless meetings and countless corporate emails, we are getting more done in fewer hours now versus yesteryear.

Dr. Martin Luther King, Jr famously said, "The arc of the moral universe is long, but it bends toward justice." Something similar can be said about the world, its people, and the businesses and organizations they create. Our march toward equality, prosperity, and peace is imperfect, lurching, and inconsistent, but it trends over prolonged periods toward progress.

Investing today is a vote for a brighter tomorrow; a practical expression of confidence that the future will be more prosperous than the present, and there is a great deal of data to support that optimism.

THE BEST WAY TO LEARN ABOUT MONEY IS TO TEACH ABOUT MONEY

EVEN THE CASUAL student of human behavior will be vaguely aware of overconfidence, the tendency to think that we are luckier, more talented, and more prescient about the future than our peers.

In *Behavioural Investing: A Practitioner's Guide to Applying Behavioural Finance*, author James Montier reports that over 95% of people think they have a better-than-average sense of humor. Peters and Waterman's *In Search of Excellence* cited that 100% of men surveyed believed they were above average interpersonally and that 94% of men viewed themselves as athletically superior to the average dude.

Overconfidence plagues us from an early age. In *The Laws of Wealth*, I cite research that American high school students rank merely as mediocre, but when those same students were questioned about how confident they were in their mathematical abilities, they lead the world. In his book *Backstage Wall Street*, Josh Brown, CEO of Ritholtz Wealth Management and a regular on CNBC, commented on the hubris in the study's findings, stating, "While there is probably something to be said for self-confidence in general, the combination of mathematical mediocrity paired with overconfidence is a significant issue in the investment world today."

It's common wisdom that overconfidence runs deep in our society, but what's less understood is just how bad it really is—the tendency is perhaps the granddaddy of all biases. Nobel laureate Daniel Kahneman referred to it as "the most significant of the cognitive biases," and says that a failure to recognize our own overconfidence keeps us from beginning on a journey of financial self-improvement.

Just as in addiction recovery, the first step is acknowledging that there is a problem, yet those who are overconfident often overlook the very factors that hinder their progress. Fortunately, there exists a dependable approach to reveal our blind spots—one that's free, simple, and as old as time itself: teaching.

Famed physicist Richard Feynman had a powerful method underscoring the difference between what we think we know and what we actually know. Feynman was a Nobel laureate esteemed for his contributions to quantum mechanics and quantum electrodynamics. I'd say this guy knew his craft cold.

He was invited to teach at Caltech in the 1960s, and took them up on the offer. Feynman was a world-renowned brainiac, but he had another arrow in his professional quiver—he quickly recognized the limitations of his understanding when he took to the teaching lectern and chalkboard. He found that explaining complex concepts to novice students required something different than expertise—reverting to the fundamentals of physics revealed gaps in his own knowledge base.

Throughout his teaching tenure, he realized he simply took some aspects of his field for granted. Humbling moments in the classroom led him to regularly go back and study again what he thought he already knew. That fundamental reset motivated Feynman to explore topics in new and different ways. Ultimately, the humility of teaching inspired him to offer ground-breaking insights and research advancements.

Feynman unknowingly contributed significantly to behavioral economics. Upon realizing gaps in his knowledge, he constructed a four-part process to identify and surmount these deficits that also serves to mitigate overconfidence:[152]

1. SELECT A CONCEPT TO LEARN

You can delve into anything. Whether it's a familiar concept or something totally new, so long as you are at least mildly interested, you can get engaged with online resources and even artificial intelligence to get up to speed. Write down everything there is to know about the subject and then break it down by its components to understand it through and through.

2. TEACH IT TO A NOVICE

This is the intimidating part for most people. While you can teach to an imaginary audience, it works better to instruct a real person—they will be able to give you feedback and ask questions that will test the boundaries of your understanding. This will identify holes in your knowledge.

3. REVIEW AND FILL GAPS
IN YOUR KNOWLEDGE

After getting slayed by your ruthless pupils, it's time to go back to your workstation and wonder why you are even doing this. Or, as the Feynman Technique outlines, gather yourself and intensely focus on the gaps the audience shed light on. The goal here is to turn weaknesses into strengths.

4. SIMPLIFY FURTHER AND
REDUCE CLUTTER

Just being an expert does not suffice. To teach, you must relate concepts in a way that a five-year-old can understand. As Feynman found, this step is critical to testing your true grasp of any subject area and it can lead you down new paths.

The Feynman Technique is rooted in something we see consistently when studying overconfidence: Specificity is the enemy of ego.

What do I mean by this?

Suppose I asked you if you thought you were intelligent. Odds are, you'd answer in the affirmative. But what if I asked if you saw yourself as smart when it comes to math? You might respond with, "Eh, well maybe I'm just OK." Now I'm going to drill down further and ask about your skills in linear algebra. If you are like most people, now you're really sweating.

When faced with a vague question like, "Am I decent with money?" most of us will likewise think, "Yeah, I'm probably at least as good as the next person," all while remaining blissfully unaware of the considerable gaps in our knowledge and their impact on our efforts to save, invest, and give in intelligent ways.

By teaching a concept to a child, friend, or co-worker, we make the discussion far more specific and are better able to spot gaps in our understanding and take pains to remedy them. Better still, this sets in place a positive cycle that not only deepens our own understanding but also allows us to impart the gift of financial literacy to others within our social circle.

OWN YOUR OUTCOMES

A**S AN ALABAMIAN**, I have always been proud to share a home state with Helen Keller, whose story of overcoming adversity teaches us about the power of radical responsibility.

At just 19 months old, Helen was afflicted with an illness, believed to have been scarlet fever or meningitis, which left her both deaf and blind. Keller faced a difficult road ahead in her isolated world of darkness and silence. Most of us would have relegated ourselves to making it a goal to survive one day at a time.

Take that in for a moment.

Put the book down and listen intently to the world around you. What do you hear?

Gaze out the nearest window. What do you see?

Capture all the details. After a minute of this exercise, imagine all of that richness fading to gray in a slow hush.

It's a depressing and frightening thought.

It's understandable that Keller would routinely lash out with anger during her early years. Extreme temper tantrums were the result of being unable to effectively express herself or comprehend the world around her. Feeling trapped in a dark and silent existence, she relied on others to complete mundane tasks for her. Over time, though, with the help of a trusted teacher, she took ownership of her life. One by one, those same chores were reclaimed by Keller, hardships notwithstanding.

Anne Sullivan, the influential instructor in Keller's life, exemplified unwavering patience and boundless compassion as she stood by Keller's side. The teacher channeled Keller's emotions to get her to overcome her communication barriers. Over the years, anger was transformed into determination. Fear turned into power. Success came one small accomplishment at a time.

In a famous quote Keller said, "No pessimist ever discovered the secrets of the stars, or sailed to an uncharted land, or opened a new heaven to the human spirit." By adopting this stance of radical responsibility, Keller eventually achieved extraordinary feats. She became the first deaf-blind person to earn a BA degree, authored several books, and won the highest civilian honor, the Presidential Medal of Freedom, while inspiring people all over the world.

The psychological term for how much control someone feels they have over their life is 'locus of control'. There are two types: internal locus of control (ILOC) and external locus of control (ELOC). Keller's transformation from external to internal locus of control was pivotal in her journey from bitterness and anger to becoming a global inspiration. Similarly, believing in your own ability to improve your life has a significant positive influence on your financial well-being.

A 2016 paper titled "Locus of Control and Savings" analyzed the relationship between individuals' locus of control and their savings behavior (wealth accumulation, saving rates, and investment allocation decisions). The researchers found that households in which the person running family finances possessed an internal locus of control tended to save more—both in absolute terms and as a proportion of their permanent incomes—compared to households with an individual with an external locus of control.[153]

Dr. Sarah Fallaw, co-author of *The Next Millionaire Next Door: Enduring Strategies for Building Wealth*, and founder of behavioral finance consultancy DataPoints, noted an expected pattern in the research: Wealthier households exhibited the greatest disparity in absolute terms between internal locus of control and external locus of control, whereas the disparity was most significant proportionally in the poorest households.

"In this latter group of poorer households, internal locus of control households enjoyed on average 40%–60% more accumulated wealth than the external locus of control households," wrote Tim Fallaw of DataPoints.[154] The findings underscore the significant impact of locus of control on wealth accumulation, particularly among households with lower socioeconomic status.

Dr. Fallaw went on to say, "Our research at DataPoints indicates a strong positive correlation between an internal locus of control and positive wealth outcomes." Fallaw further writes in the aforementioned book, "Those who are financially independent focus on their own choices, taking responsibility for their money-related actions and behaviors."

That is somewhat of a hot take in today's personal finance discourse. Research and assertions like the above tend to upset some people because, well, life circumstances can be brutally unfair. It's absolutely true that a fortunate few get a massive head start, while others face substantial financial hurdles. Heck, some lucky individuals are born an inch from the finish line!

It's undeniable that certain segments of the population grow up in households and communities where positive lessons about money are more available than others. A sound mind, a trust fund, a parent who is a legacy graduate of a university, a drama-free household with a grasp of basic financial literacy... all these advantages provide an early financial edge in life that cannot be easily standardized. Injustice and bad luck exist—both systematic and random—and the playing field will never be completely level, although we should strive for such equality.

But this is where Dr. Fallaw counsels us to carefully distinguish between "things that don't make me happy" and "things that aren't true." All of the wrongs I just mentioned do nothing to change the simple fact that taking personal responsibility for your financial life leads to dramatically better outcomes than accepting the alternative.

———————

Carol Dweck, psychologist and co-author of *Mindset: The New Psychology of Success*, underscores the importance of developing a growth attitude, which aligns closely with the concept of an internal locus of control. Her ideas can help us take ownership of our lives, no matter where along the path we started. Here are some of her actionable takeaways, as applied to your money life:

- **Embrace the power of 'yet'**: Replace 'can't' with 'can't yet' in your vocabulary when you face tough projects at work or the thought of never being able to retire. Just as you become more skilled on the job with each passing week and notch up valuable experiences, growing your wealth is often an agonizingly slow process. While you are not yet there, you will be with the right planning and behavior.
- **Effort is the path to mastery**: Even the most talented athletes must practice to achieve greatness. Developing sound habits and working hard can be the equalizers if you lack savvy saving or investing habits. Just by doing some of the right things with consistency and a bit of grunt work, long-term financial success is within reach.
- **Seek constructive feedback**: Welcome input from others as an opportunity to learn and grow. That might mean talking with a

financial advisor or openly conversing with trusted individuals about your relationship with money. Criticism can serve as a catalyst for self-improvement and personal development.

- **Emphasize the process over the outcome**: It's all about the climb, so the pop song says. Enjoy the journey and fulfillment of personal growth by shifting your focus from solely chasing end results. If you reach a near- or intermediate-term goal, go ahead and reward yourself. You have my permission. Also, accept that the occasional setback will happen.
- **Cultivate a love of learning**: Foster a mindset of continuous learning by viewing new challenges as opportunities for personal growth. Successful retirees often embrace activities and ideas that they never thought would become part of their lives. Be open to exploring new experiences and expanding your horizons.

Your past mistakes and current flaws don't define you. Take ownership of your future and adopt a growth mindset to overcome all challenges you face—be they financial or otherwise. Start taking control of your money journey today.

YOUR PAST, PRESENT, AND FUTURE CAN ALL MAKE YOU BETTER WITH MONEY

A Christmas Carol BY Charles Dickens is in my top ten favorite and most important books. It is an existential masterpiece that is not always seen as such because of its ubiquity and the seemingly endless film adaptations.

The novella centers around Ebenezer Scrooge, a miserly man who only cares about money and rejects the spirit of Christmas. One Christmas Eve, he's visited by three spirits, each showing him the consequences of his selfishness along with the importance of love and kindness.

The three ghosts that visit Scrooge transform his life, reshape his behavior, and serve as a template for thinking about how a tour of the various times of our lives can be rich with learning. Just like Scrooge, we can confront our financial ghosts of past, present, and future en route to living a rich life.

The Past: First to arrive at Scrooge's bedside is the Ghost of Christmas Past. This trip takes the bitter man to his youth. Young Ebenezer endured a lonely and neglected childhood, which included the loss of a family member and estrangement from his one true love, Belle, due to his obsession with wealth. By vividly recalling the events that molded the person he had become, he begins to recognize how his experiences led him to become such an ornery old man. Any positive memories brought up evoke only feelings of remorse and regret.

The Present: Next up is the Ghost of Christmas Present. Primed with an understanding of why he's not exactly a jolly old soul during the holiday season, Scrooge is shown scenes of joy others experience in the current Christmastime, while he lacks any semblance of cheer. The heartwarming image of the Cratchit family, despite their humble circumstances, leaves a lasting impression. Moreover, the touching moments with Tiny Tim evoke deep emotions. Scrooge's cold and detached behaviors are contrasted with the spirit's lessons about the value of family, love, and compassion in the present moment. His heart softens just a bit more, and he begins to wonder what all his wealth is for.

The Future: Finally, the Ghost of Christmas Yet to Come takes on a different aura. This time, Ebenezer encounters his own demise, with nobody there to mourn his passing. What's worse, though, is the devastation he feels witnessing the tragic death of Tiny Tim. It's a revelation of the man's mortality along with the potential impact he could have on others. In a moment of awakening, he realizes the emptiness of his current life path and legacy.

Dickens uses the past, present, and future as catalysts for introspection, effectively showing how Scrooge's behavior is deeply rooted in his life experiences. The trip through time allows him to understand the consequences of his actions and attitudes, prompting Scrooge to undergo a profound transformation. He soon embraces Christmas with actions of compassion and generosity.

Ultimately, Dickens emphasizes a pivotal message: Scrooge owns his current and future behaviors and attitudes; who he is today does not define who he can become. Redemption is possible for everyone—even the rich.

———————

Perhaps it's time to embark on a journey of your own self-rediscovery, forging new ways to make a positive impact on the lives of your loved ones and beyond.

Will you choose to delve into your past, present, and future selves? Each of these three parts of our life bears unique insights and lessons if we are ready to listen and learn. From the past we should seek understanding, from the present connection, and from the future inspiration.

Brendan Frazier, an expert in all things of the human side of money, has this to say about a focus on the past: "Most financial advice revolves around two points in life:

1. Where you are today (present)
2. Where you want to be (future)

Yet, a client's attitudes, beliefs, and behaviors driving their financial decisions are derived from the one area not listed. The past."[155]

Frazier provides an example of an individual whose parents demonstrated love through expensive gifts, and now she unwittingly repeats that pattern. A lavish lifestyle works to the detriment of achieving her savings goals, as she neglects saving for tomorrow.

He says: "A belief formed in the past influenced her decision-making in the present that jeopardized her goals for the future. The best advice focuses on the past, present, and future."

It is important to make a distinction here that can be lost in the sometimes deterministic world of backward-looking psychology: Your past has indeed influenced who you are today, sometimes significantly, but it does not dictate all that you can become (see Scrooge).

The point of exhuming past financial decisions and narratives is to examine them, identify which ones are still relevant, and make more conscious decisions today and tomorrow. It is never about wallowing in past mistakes or letting money scripts with which we were raised dictate our financial behaviors moving forward. As Freud once said, "Not to know the past is to be in bondage to it, while to remember, to know, is to be set free."

To begin to understand your past, ask yourself the following:

- What are my earliest memories about money, and what is the impact of those memories on my current financial decision-making?
- What financial setbacks and successes have I experienced in the past, and what can they teach me about a brighter future?
- What themes or patterns are present when I look back at my money decisions over the years, and what experiences or scripts might be driving these decisions?

Ponder those right now as we go back in time.

In the early 1800s, Soren Kierkegaard observed, "Most men pursue pleasure with such breathless haste that they hurry past it."

It would seem that not much has changed since Kierkegaard's time, with the average American today spending $18,000 annually on non-essential expenses.[156] Now, there's nothing wrong with discretionary spending per se (our economy depends on it and I certainly do my share), but a great deal of that spending happens beneath our awareness and without our enjoyment, which is a problem.

Furthermore, a survey of more than 1,000 respondents found that people, on average, waste $139 a month on unnecessary fees, repeated purchases, and forgotten monthly subscriptions (not to mention that stack of unused gift cards you have lying somewhere). While this may not seem like much, the opportunity cost over a lifetime is significant. Assuming careless expenses of $139/month, a working lifetime of 43 years, and an average return of 10% per year in a stock index fund, that money would compound to over a million dollars if invested and saved each month instead of being wasted!

Spending money and treating ourselves to luxury goods is not inherently bad. I think we can all agree, though, that we can do a better job of spending more consciously while savoring the value of the money that we use. That is the goal of the present.

So, to self-assess your progress, ask yourself the following:

- How often do I take a moment to appreciate what I already have before thinking about what I want to buy next?
- Have I recently examined my spending in detail to ensure no 'leakage', such as redundant or unused purchases?
- What emotions arise when I think about money, and how do these emotions impact how I spend?

Having now learned the lessons of the past, and to embrace living in the present, it's time for us to build a vision for the future that inspires bold action.

Here, the work of Viktor Frankl's 'Logotherapy' is powerfully applicable. For background, logotherapy is a psychotherapy that emphasizes finding purpose in life. We can harness its power to help you make more meaningful and fulfilling financial decisions by aligning your spending with your values. This technique encourages conscious actions that can lead to a greater sense of contentment.

Whereas Freudian determinism says that we are pushed by our past (thanks for nothing, Mom and Dad), Frankl posits that we can instead be pulled forward by our dreams for the future. The former is completely out of our hands, but the latter is well within our control.

Frankl observed firsthand in the concentration camps that, "The prisoner who had lost faith in the future—his future—was doomed. With his loss of belief in the future, he also lost his spiritual hold; he let himself decline and became subject to physical and mental decay." Breaking with the psychoanalytic traditions of his day, Frankl set forth a bold, empowering vision of human thriving, saying, "It isn't the past which holds us back, it's the future; and how we undermine it, today."

For all of us, our financial future suffers when we allow ourselves to be bound by the money stories of childhood or past mistakes. We undermine our financial future when we become so mired in the grind of daily life that we never lift our eyes to imagine the life that could exist just over the horizon.

Creating a compelling vision for our money future isn't mere woo-woo vision-boarding nonsense; it is a proven means for streaming decision-making and catalyzing action.

If your future vision seems cloudy, reflect on these questions:

- What does financial success mean to me in the most personal terms, and how does it look different for me compared to my friends or family?
- What impact do I want to have on the world, and how would more wealth help bring that mission to pass?
- What personal and financial risks have I been hesitant to take, and how could calculated risks taken today lead to a more abundant tomorrow?

Remember, just like Frankl's powerful insights and Scrooge's transformative experience, we have it in us to create and live out a brighter future by aligning our aspirations with purposeful choices. When it comes to our money, we must be intentional, strive to make an impact, and never be timid about taking a few risks.

MONEY CAN BUY
HAPPINESS WHEN YOU
SPEND IT CORRECTLY

THE LATE 19TH century featured some of the most charismatic and driven industrial tycoons in American lore. On the Mount Rushmore of bold entrepreneurs of that era is Andrew Carnegie. At one point, Carnegie had climbed the money mountain to surpass John D. Rockefeller as America's richest person.

We associate Carnegie and his family with vast sums of wealth and noble philanthropic initiatives, but his life began with humble beginnings.

Carnegie was born into a poor family in Scotland in 1835. His father struggled to provide for the family amid difficult economic conditions in the country. The Carnegie clan decided to borrow money and move to America. They settled in Allegheny, Pennsylvania in 1848. From there, Andrew began work changing spools in a cotton mill 12 hours a day, six days a week, earning him a weekly paycheck of $42 (and that is adjusted for inflation).

Carnegie was in the right place at the right time, though. Allegheny, later annexed by Pittsburgh, would become Steel City.

It was in that thriving city and industry where Carnegie's fortune was forged.

Cementing his legacy, however, was his philosophy of philanthropy. Following the sale of his steel company to J. P. Morgan in 1901, Carnegie devoted the rest of his life to giving away his wealth for the good of society. The extent of the man's generosity is incredible.

Perhaps Carnegie's most significant contribution to the public was the establishment of libraries. He loved books. He took $60 million of his fortune to fund a system of 1,689 public libraries across the country.[157] Imagine how many children to this day have fallen in love with reading at a Carnegie library.

Carnegie believed that education was vital for a better world. In 1900, he donated $1 million (about $36 million today) to create a technical institute for the city of Pittsburgh. He envisioned a school where working-class people could learn practical skills.[158]

The list goes on. His humanitarian efforts and love of the arts are seen in the Carnegie Hero Fund he helped establish and—what many New Yorkers and tourists might know him best for—the Carnegie Hall concert center. He even funded altruistic efforts through the Carnegie Endowment of International Peace, which has a mission to promote understanding and diplomatic solutions to global conflict.

These examples represent just a fraction of his philanthropic initiatives. All told, he donated more than $350 million over his lifetime, equivalent to more than $10 billion today, and his impact lives on. We are all the beneficiaries of his legacy.

Carnegie's philanthropy is best summed up in his most famous quote, "Wealth is not to feed our egos but to feed the hungry and to help people help themselves." He truly embodied another well-known saying of his: "The man who dies thus rich dies disgraced."

So, did money make Andrew Carnegie happy?

Well, I didn't get the chance to ask him personally, but it certainly seems as though the answer is, "yes." This affirmative conclusion is far less about the vastness of his fortune and a great deal more to do with how he chose to spend it. Money, if used correctly, can indeed provide us with happiness.

Elizabeth Dunn, a professor of psychology at the University of British Columbia, and Michael Norton, a business professor at Harvard, did extensive research on this topic. In their book, *Happy Money: The Science of Happier Spending*, five spending areas are identified as being proven to provide the greatest contentment.

1. Spending on experiences
2. Spending on others
3. Buying time
4. Bypassing materialism
5. Funding life's necessities

The relationship between money and happiness is complex, but evidence shows that the more we invest in cool and fun experiences, preferably with friends and family, the better off we'll be compared to accumulating stuff. Also, like Carnegie, donating your time and financial resources often delivers dividends of peace and joy, not only to others but also to yourself. And if you are a busy parent, consider hiring someone to complete household chores and the like—that effectively buys you more time with your spouse and kids.

The fourth item on the list relates to point one: Not much happiness is gained from pursuing material possessions solely for the sake of status—you'll be left with a pile of stress rather than a joy-filled heart. Finally, a little wealth goes a long way; simply being able to not worry about making ends meet offers peace of mind (something many of us may take for granted).

The point: Dunn and Norton's conclusions underscore that how we use money ultimately determines its impact on our well-being.

Another tip for squeezing the most joy from your money is to treat yourself when you accomplish a major life milestone or finish an annoying little task. Whether it's a family celebration at a nice restaurant or just getting through a busy week and reaching for your favorite bottle of wine, focusing on turning the small things into a treat makes them all that more special. That might mean cutting back on spending in certain areas for a while.

Something else you should target is to align your spending with your personality. A 2016 study by Sandra Matz, Joe Gladstone, and David Stillwell found that individual differences play a central role in determining the 'right' spending methods to boost our mental welfare. Research on 76,000 bank transaction records was used, and the authors concluded that people whose purchases matched their personality type reported higher levels of life satisfaction.[159] So, an extroverted person might very well have their life improved by joining a social club in ways that it wouldn't if they had bought, say, an expensive bobble.

In another chapter, I made the bold statement that money kinda, sorta buys happiness sometimes, unless it doesn't. So brave! It turns out, though, that some of money's ability to buy happiness is in our hands, and that the joy we do or don't experience has a great deal to do with how we choose to spend.

When Dr. Michael Finke joined me on my podcast, he shared a contrarian take. According to him, investing in something like an expensive car could potentially bring happiness in retirement, but not just any car—specifically, the type of car that grants entry into the rarified world of car clubs. As Dr. Finke stated on the show, it's not the set of wheels itself that brings delight and thrills.

Rather, what the car facilitates is the acquisition of a group of like-minded friends and the ability to drink coffee and talk about V12s on Saturdays in the summer.

Again and again, we see that money is best spent in ways that deepen our humanity and connectedness to others. Money can buy you a huge house and tracts of land that isolate you, but it can also afford you the ability to bless the lives of others, experience new things, and bond with friends around a shared passion.

The choice is yours; will you use money to connect? Or to isolate yourself in a gilded cage of loneliness?

YOU ARE YOUR
BEST INVESTMENT

Mary Anning was a pioneering paleontologist of the early 19th century. She was known around the world for her discoveries of Jurassic marine fossil beds along the English Channel.

Before gaining notoriety for her professional prowess, she endured a tough upbringing and faced countless challenges given the rigid gender stereotypes of the day. It probably didn't help that she was also struck by lightning at just 15 months old.[160]

As she grew up, Mary Anning had a fascination for collecting fossils that flourished under her father's guidance. However, her formal educational opportunities were limited due to the state of girls' and women's education at the time. As an adult, Anning faced societal restrictions that hindered her chances of intellectual and professional advancement, as opportunities for women were scarce.

With the help of her father and an internal drive to learn more, she gained expertise in paleontology through hands-on lessons in the field along with isolated studies, even though it was downright odd for an English woman to pursue such an intellectually rigorous passion at that time.

WARNING: The next few paragraphs are going to make you feel like a bit of an underachiever.

Mary Anning left an indelible mark on her field despite scant classroom education and significant cultural barriers. She discovered many marine reptiles, and at age 12 (yes, 12!) unearthed a 5.2-meter-long ichthyosaur skeleton—people were reportedly convinced that she had dug up a monster.

Throughout her career, Mary Anning continued to make numerous significant fossil discoveries, among them the first complete Plesiosaurus specimen, which furthered the understanding of geological theories. Her work played a crucial role in the scientific community's growing comprehension of the concept of extinction and the use of fossils as evidence of ancient life forms. Despite the ongoing underestimation of her male counterparts, Anning's research was featured in major scientific publications, solidifying her legacy as a ground-breaking paleontologist.

Anning passed away at age 47, but her remarkable story continues to capture the imagination of scientific communities and wider society. She is now remembered as not only a revolutionary in paleontology, but also a trailblazer for women's progress.

Let's return to the present and the future: How would you perform in your craft given such uphill battles? What skills and traits would you focus on today to build a better professional tomorrow?

Mary Anning lived an incredible life and made significant contributions because she understood the importance of curiosity and constant self-improvement, even in the face of long odds. Although every externality was working against her, Mary bet on herself and won big. As you will soon see, this is an attitude that will greatly benefit those seeking to build wealth.

When people learn that I work in finance, the questions that follow (assuming they have not run away screaming) are always very similar.

"What do you think the market will do this year?"

"What do you think (ABC political event) will do to the market?"

"Do you think (XYZ world concern) will tank the market?"

In addition to being fundamentally unknowable, these sorts of questions share in common that they are totally out of our control, ignoring the reality that investment success starts within.

One of the most insidious forms of this 'looking outside' is trying to beat the market. It's understandably appealing—trading securities requires little actual effort, can be done at zero cost, and has the potential for incredible upside. And each year, there are a handful of stocks that shoot to the moon, further enticing people to roll the dice in the speculation game.

The idea of generating meaningful wealth by hand-selecting shares remains a myth for just about everyone, even professionals. Each year, S&P Dow Jones Indices produces a recap of how well active mutual fund managers performed relative to their respective benchmarks. Or shall we say, how poorly they performed. Through year-end 2022, 93.4% of all large-cap funds failed to match or exceed the S&P 500's total return over the previous 15 years.[161] So, less than 7% of professional investors—people who have trained to do this their whole lives and have the top tools of the trade—beat the market.

And *you* have the audacity to think you're going to make this happen in your pajamas from your laptop? Not a high-probability shot, my friend.

But take heart. There is a much more reliable path to wealth, and we can look to Mary Anning as a guide: Wager on yourself.

While few individuals spoke of personal finance principles two centuries ago (were there even such things as finance gurus back then?), we can quantify just how lucrative an education can be.

Consider that the median household annual income for a high school graduate is about $50,000. Earn a college degree, and the expected salary is roughly $106,000, while Ph.D.s command

$162,000. Now, let's go crazy and assume the additional income from just a single year is invested at 10% annually for 50 years. The college graduate's account would be worth more than $6.5 million, and Dr. Smarty-pants would have a nest egg close to $13 million. Sure, there are costs such as tuition, taxes, and the like, but you get the picture. A bet on yourself can be incredibly lucrative.

While doing extra semesters in the classroom is the most intuitive form of investing in self, there are other actions you can take to improve your well-being. Diet and exercise, finding a mentor, journaling, breaking a bad habit, or going to therapy—each of these actions has an upside that is valuable on its own, but many of them also have financial rewards, sweetening an already worthwhile undertaking. Research proves these three behaviors should have a spot on your financial plan and investment policy statement:

1. **Exercise regularly**: According to a study featured in the BMJ *Open Sport & Exercise Medicine Journal*, habitually working out can result in nearly $2,000 per year in reduced healthcare spending.[162] What fun could you have with an extra couple grand in your yearly budget?

2. **See a therapist**: Men will literally trade meme stocks rather than go to therapy. While you may or may not score with the former, the latter has been shown to increase income for men by 12.4% annually, according to 2018 data published in the *European Economic Review*. Women experience future wage gains of 8.1%.[163]

3. **Find a mentor or be a mentor**: Young workers with an experienced colleague guiding them along stand a better chance of loftier pay raises and promotions compared to their non-mentored peers. What's more, senior managers and business owners also benefit financially from encouraging mentor programs on the job.[164] So, if you're a Marty McFly, go find your Doc Brown.

Whether through education, improved mental health, increased fitness, or getting the guidance of a wise mentor, self-improvement is a reliable path to a better life, and oh yeah, a lot more money along the way.

We often seek an external silver-bullet fix for our finances, hoping to find the perfect stock, time the market, and achieve financial freedom effortlessly. But entrusting our success to the whims of actively trading volatile markets that embarrass CFA-credentialed Ivy League experts with great regularity is a formula for frustration and disappointment.

The true path to success lies in taking charge of your destiny by investing in your own personal growth and development. To map it out, ask yourself:

- What is an area of my life in which I could invest to further my growth?
- What is an enjoyable means by which self-improvement could occur?
- What is the smallest first step I could take in the direction of this new me?

You can't count on a bolt of lightning to power a DeLorean or jumpstart your finances. Instead, take a cue from Mary Anning—identify areas in your life where you can plant a seed for growth and see where that growth takes you.

YOUR MOST
IMPORTANT FINANCIAL
DECISIONS AREN'T
FINANCIAL AT ALL

G IVEN THAT MONEY is such a worry for most of us, it makes
sense that many of us daydream of what it might be like to
have been born rich.

But even a brief examination of the lives of those born rich or
famous shows that it's not quite as simple or as desirable as it might
seem from a distance. It is no mistake that one of the narratives
that runs through every form of wisdom tradition is, "be careful
what you wish for because you just might get it."

Don't believe me?

Let me introduce you to Barbara Hutton, once one of America's
richest women. Born in 1912 to Edna Woolworth, daughter of F. W.
Woolworth (founder of the famous chain of five-and-dime stores)
and Laws Hutton, a wealthy businessperson, she had it made. As
a result of troubled aspects of her personal life, however, she would

be later known as "The Poor Little Rich Girl." You see, the way she acquired her wealth was quite tragic. At the age of five her mother died, some say from suicide, leaving Barbara with an inheritance in the tens of millions.

Her financial follies began at age 21 when she married Prince Alexis Mdivani, a European aristocrat. That match turned south in short order, ending in divorce after just two years in 1935. Mdivani was quite the spendthrift—he was known to use his wife's cash to throw lavish parties, and he constantly gambled. He was unfaithful both financially and within their marriage.

In all, Hutton was married and divorced seven times, including to a baron, three princes, a count, a playboy, and actor Cary Grant (earning them the nickname "Cash 'n' Cary" in the press).

Compounding her money woes was a proclivity to always want to financially support her friends and an ongoing struggle with substance abuse. Hutton died at age 66 in her penthouse suite at the Beverly Wilshire Hotel in Beverly Hills, California. Once wealthy, she passed away on the verge of bankruptcy.

Even after inheriting today's equivalent of $2 billion, she had just a few thousand in the bank in her final years. And let's be blunt: A lousy taste in men took a toll on her financial solvency. While most people wouldn't consider choosing the wrong partner a financial wellness risk, it cost Barbara billions. For instance, according to a 2017 feature, her 53-day marriage with Porfirio Rubirosa got off to an expensive start—she gifted "Rubi" a check for $1 million and the following items: a coffee plantation in the Dominican Republic, a B-25 plane, polo ponies, jewelry, oh, and a final $2.5 million settlement check.[165]

––––––––––

The fact is money touches every part of our lives. Consequently, the decisions we make in every area inevitably affect our finances.

We might not have billions to lose in our own relationships, but regardless of personal wealth, the financial cost of divorce is staggering.

According to a 2005 study, the household income of a child's family typically drops by 42% following a divorce—statistically comparable to the decline of the U.S. economy during the Great Depression, impacting both the parents and children. You see, when a couple divorces, the strong joint economy of the mother and father splits into two separate and weaker economies. The result is a significantly reduced post-divorce wealth level.[166] Likewise disturbing, almost half of American families fall into poverty after a divorce, per research by Julia Heath and B. F. Kiker.[167] The Organization for Economic Cooperation and Development (OECD) reports that three-in-four women applying for welfare benefits do so because of a disrupted relationship.[168]

And while the emotional wounds of divorce typically heal, money traumas can endure—a Fidelity study found that five years after splitting up, 75% of divorcées said they were emotionally back in a good place, but only 65% said they had financially recovered.[169] Given all this, it's not a shocker that divorce is the greatest predictor of the length of poverty spells, according to Heath and Kiker.

We would like to think of love as this pure thing that remains unbesmirched by money, but it's clear that having more money makes staying in love easier, and staying in love leads to having more money. Likewise, decisions such as where to live, who to love, what to study, and what to eat all have a material impact on our wealth, even though none of them would make it into a financial literacy course.

Here are some tips for evaluating decisions of all stripes in a way that leads to greater wealth in the most holistic sense:

- **Employ the 10/10/10 rule**: Weigh the ramifications of your decisions in the short term (ten minutes), medium term (ten months), and long term (ten years). Sort of like how Jerry Seinfeld is constantly fighting 'night guy' and 'morning guy', mentally separating out immediate pleasure from possible longer-term regret helps you make wiser choices in the present.
- **Try reverse thinking**: Instead of immediately asking, "What should I do?" try considering, "What should I avoid?" or "What would be the worst decision?" Sticking with our marriage example, reflecting on the traits one might want to avoid, and recognizing red flags in a potential partner, can lead to more informed and thoughtful decisions. This strategy might uncover hidden risks and maybe even identify better alternatives.
- **Examine the decision from different angles**: Emotional (What do I want to do?), practical (What makes the most sense to do?), critical (Why might this not make sense?), and vanishing options (What would I do if this option were no longer available to me?). This multi-dimensional approach provides a comprehensive understanding of potential impacts.
- **Run a small-scale experiment**: My wife, before she agreed to marry me (you'll have to ask her how that decision has worked out), surreptitiously ran several little experiments to see if I was *the one*. Here's what I mean: She invited me on an extended family vacation to Bryce Canyon National Park to see how I interacted with kids (she has a much younger brother), how I handled limited sleep, if she would grow tired of my company on a road trip, and if I could connect with her many different family members' personalities as well as flex to meet them where they were at. It turned out I had the right stuff. These experiences allowed her to make an informed decision based on real information rather than merely relying on assumptions.

It is a mistake to view life in overly binary terms of financial versus non-financial aspects. By thinking in more integrated ways, we gain the ability to make decisions with the appropriate perspective and gravity.

Putting into practice the techniques mentioned here, such as considering various angles, running experiments on loved ones (I'm still surprised I passed the test), and examining potential risks enables us to make well-informed choices. Money influences life, and life influences money, but your influence is the most powerful of all.

THE MOST
POWERFUL WORDS
IN INVESTING

P RESIDENT LINCOLN WAS already an accomplished person
when he took the oath of office. A skilled lawyer and veteran
of political campaigning, Honest Abe knew how to assess a playing
field. Maybe more importantly, he knew when to call on his advisors
and other mentors when his knowledge was not up to snuff.

It's an understatement to describe January 1861 as a challenging
time for the young nation Lincoln was about to preside over.
Recognizing the daunting task of being a war-time president (a
civil war, no less), he sought the counsel of experts and others he
knew to hold different beliefs from his own. Members of Lincoln's
cabinet were a motley crew, some even being his staunchest
critics and rivals.

What made the 16th president effective during such a tumultuous
time was his humility. By acknowledging his own limitations and
admitting "I don't know" when faced with tough choices and
strategy, he and his team were able to guide the country through
the Civil War.

Team of Rivals, a book by historian Doris Kearns Goodwin,

delves into Lincoln's thought processes and how he sought to unite a divided nation, not by dismissing contrary opinions, but by embracing them. Lincoln's success was less about knowing everything and more about identifying what he did not know, and then surrounding himself with the people who could fill in those gaps.

And the rest is history.

————————

If conceding a lack of expertise was good enough for President Lincoln, it's something all of us should try to apply to our daily lives and our finances.

It has been said that the most *dangerous* words in investing are, "This time is different." I'd like to suggest that the most *powerful* words in investing are, "I don't know."

The psychological term for knowing what you know and what you don't know is *metaknowledge*—literally, knowledge about knowledge. It includes several facets.

First, being aware of our cognitive biases is crucial. Metaknowledge involves an awareness of biases and heuristics that influence how we make decisions. The more we know about these biases, the better equipped we are to mitigate their effects. For example, let's say you get emotional about financial matters and have difficulty watching the daily zigs and zags of the markets. Knowing this about yourself, you are free to make decisions that will decrease the likelihood that this discomfort will derail your long-term goals. For instance, you may willingly choose to check your portfolio less frequently, as doing so may set off a series of impulsive actions that could mess up your financial plan. Or you may choose to work with a professional to provide you with steady guidance and a calming perspective in tough times. While you may never be a financial wunderkind yourself, your metaknowledge of your own shortcomings has effectively rendered the need for these advanced abilities obsolete by avoiding panic altogether.

Next, it's key to admit you just don't know it all. Metaknowledge incorporates the reality that knowledge is always shifting. Think about your career—how different is it today compared to ten years ago? What are the things you once knew that just ain't so? What do you know now that wasn't true before? The truth is that knowledge is always evolving, and there are constant tweaks to truth itself.

When it comes to investment markets and what your financial future holds, there is so much that is unknowable.

To pick just one example among a host of perennial failures, let's take a look at what the experts predicted stocks would do in 2008. According to Bespoke Investments, on January 2, 2008, the average Wall Street strategist's year-end price target was 1632 (which would have put the index of large-cap U.S. stocks at an all-time high).[170] The index closed the year at 903. Perhaps forecasting is better left to the meteorologists.

If markets are unpredictable, so are budget-busting events in your personal life. Unexpected costs such as those related to caring for an elderly parent, a major health scare, and putting a few kids through college, among others, can be significant risks. While it's possible to plan for these potential financial burdens to some extent, you cannot simply input all the data into a spreadsheet and expect to be provided with an exact dollar amount of savings to target. We make (financial) plans, life laughs. The only realistic stance is that numerous unforeseen financial events can and will significantly affect your financial plan. Unfortunately, we are just plain bad at estimating these sorts of future risks.

Neil Weinstein, a psychology professor at Rutgers, performed a study in which he asked subjects to rate the likelihood they perceived of encountering a set of negative events, ranging from getting mugged, fired, and divorced, to developing a serious health condition (42 events in all). Other research has asked participants to rate the likelihood of a series of positive events, like winning the lottery, or getting a raise. Examining the results, there is a striking trend that shows the participants are overly optimistic about what their future may hold. We tend to own the optimistic and delegate the dangerous. We believe that we are much more likely than average to win the lottery or be lucky in love, while divorce and disease are seen as the bad luck of some other sucker. When it comes to our money, this dramatic misperception of reality leads to a number of negative sequelae, including not saving enough for a rainy day, not having adequate insurance, and unrealistic assumptions about portfolio returns.

Lastly, knowledge about where to find more knowledge is key to metaknowledge. I don't know a thing about cars. I mean, absolutely not one thing. I can't change a tire, replace a spark plug, and heaven help us all if someone let me near a brake pad. But that's OK because I know a few good mechanics near me, who I trust to do good work. The real danger lies not in me being clueless about cars, but in me thinking I know how to fix a car when I don't.

Likewise, it's perfectly fine if your financial knowledge doesn't extend much beyond the basics, so long as you know where to turn for help.

Locating the right resources is easier than ever today, but it's also fraught with more risk. You can gather guidance with a few clicks, swipes, or AI prompts, but it is often difficult to know if the advice rendered is appropriate for you.

Like Lincoln, surrounding yourself with a trusted advisor who understands you, your strengths, and your hangups, is a form of metaknowledge that can pay strong dividends. A 2019 Vanguard study, updated in 2022, estimated that a trustworthy and skilled wealth manager can add an extra three percentage points of annual return compared to you taking a DIY approach.[171] Research by Russell Investments suggests 4% of so-called "advisor alpha."[172] You don't have to know it all, you just have to know where to turn.

The entire modern economy is based around the idea of specialization, and we are all better for it, both in terms of how we spend our time and the quality of goods and services we receive. We accept for a fact that a French bakery will have better croissants than we could create at home, and that we probably shouldn't try and fix our own Rolex.

And yet, all too often, we lack metaknowledge around our pocketbooks and portfolios. Maybe we have just enough contact with money—we earn it, we spend it, we use it daily—to think that we alone can get the most from it. Yet far more important than what we know about money is our willingness to look for help as we become aware of all that we don't know.

TAKE THE WORST
CASE OFF THE TABLE

EW INDUSTRIES WERE left unscathed by the Great Financial Crisis. The 2007 to 2009 period was fraught with massive job layoffs, corporate bankruptcies, and plummeting stock prices.

Investors today might still get chills thinking about how the crisis either delayed their retirement targets or wiped out years' worth of savings and investment gains. Fear permeated the collective consciousness at that time, affecting both public and corporate leaders alike.

The auto industry was no different. It was arguably hit harder than most, given the steep rise in fuel prices and raw materials costs that took place leading up to the autumn of 2008. Car companies worldwide were forced to conjure up creative marketing campaigns to attract cautious consumers.

Amazingly, while its competitors were enduring sharp demand declines and tweaking loan rates offered to buyers, Hyundai managed to grow global unit sales and increase positive brand awareness.[173]

How did the South Korean automaker gain significant market share against the backdrop of such a dire economic reality?

It did so by taking the worst case off the table for would-be buyers.

Along with a strong product line that focused on safety, reliability, and fuel efficiency, a new out-of-the-box strategy allowed Hyundai to thrive when the industry was hurting so badly: the Hyundai Assurance Program. It will go down in corporate history as among the boldest and most successful marketing initiatives ever.

After navigating 2008 relatively well, the company introduced a new program that allowed customers to return their car, no questions asked, and with no credit score impact, if they were to lose their job. The worst case—that you'd be unable to pay your car note—had effectively been obviated.

The Hyundai Assurance Program was an instant hit. Hyundai's sales and market share in the U.S. were on the rise and it was later named Marketer of the Year by Ad Age.[174]

What made the strategy such a success was that it struck a chord with folks across the country. People were not so much afraid of paying a few extra percentage points on an auto loan rate during the GFC. Rather, it was the intense fear of losing one's job that was constantly on people's minds. Hyundai, by saying to folks, "Don't worry; if you lose your job, just return the car, no problem," relieved customers' anxiety. The company's U.S. market share jumped from 3.1% in 2008 to 4.3% through late 2009.[175] The campaign was later brought back during the Covid crisis in March and April of 2020.

Hyundai, like so many successful corporations, wasn't aiming for benevolence and altruism. It was that it did not want to let a good crisis go to waste. The Assurance Program capitalized on the human tendency to imagine the worst. "OMG, if I get laid off, I could lose my house, I'd have to go into big-time debt, and my car will get repossessed," was a common mental refrain during the GFC.

Psychologists call this 'catastrophizing'. We tend to blow potential problems out of proportion, magnifying what could go wrong and underestimating our capacity to handle those outcomes. Catastrophizing involves irrational thoughts and fears of the future, leading us to fixate on worst-case scenarios, which mucks up our ability to act rationally in the present.

There must have been some behavioral finance pros on the marketing team over at Hyundai. Not only did they have the guts to launch the strategy during the worst of the GFC, but they also paid up for pricey ads in the 2009 Super Bowl. The name itself felt like a warm blanket: the Assurance Program. Later in 2009, seven in ten Americans had a positive or neutral perception of the Hyundai brand.

———————

Shifting gears to personal finance, when we focus on what could go wrong, we can quickly veer off the right financial path. This sort of dwelling on the negative becomes cyclical, leading us to scarier and scarier places mentally, without a solution in sight.

But there is another way.

Just like Hyundai, if we take the worst financial case off the table, it can allow us to free up our headspace for more pleasant thoughts and immediately dismiss the catastrophic kind. This is accomplished by allocating a percentage of our wealth to a dedicated *safety bucket* that typically covers between six months and two years of bad times in the market without touching the rest of your wealth. Think of it as a personal finance assurance program! It's a simple solution, but as you'll see below, the results can be powerful.

The bucket approach is sometimes labeled as goals-based investing (GBI). Many in the financial advisory industry have come to embrace the notion of earmarking certain portions of a client's portfolio for specific goals and risks. A safety bucket, commonly utilized with GBI, often helps people invest more aggressively with other parts (or buckets) of their portfolio, knowing they have their worst-case scenario money put aside, so to speak. Then, whenever a bear market strikes, they are less wont to sell at the wrong time.

SEI Investments was one of the first to incorporate GBI in a systematic way. It rolled out a goals-based platform immediately before the GFC, just the right time for researchers like myself. That allowed us to observe the behavioral impact of a goals-based approach to wealth management versus traditional methods that simply compared returns to the broader market.

As I described in *Personal Benchmark*, co-authored with Brinker Capital founder Chuck Widger, we uncovered the following distinctions between the two groups:

Of those in a single, traditional investment portfolio:

- 50% chose to fully liquidate their portfolios or at least their equity portfolios, including many high-net-worth clients who had no immediate need for cash.
- 10% made significant changes in their equity allocation, reducing it by 25% or more.

Of those clients in a goals-based investment strategy:

- 75% made no changes.
- 20% decided to increase the size of their immediate needs pool, but left their longer-term assets fully invested.

The GBI method took the worst case off the table and the positive behavior followed. It's reasonable to assume that clients with that investment strategy in place felt confident that their safety bucket was ample enough to help them weather the near-term storms brought about by the GFC. As Rayer of SEI concluded, the key finding was that "goals-based investors are less likely to panic and make ill-informed changes to their portfolios."

What makes the wheels run on GBI is that, like the Hyundai Assurance Program, there are safeguards built in that play on our behavioral tendency to fear the unknown and to ruminate on all that could go wrong. There's a sharp difference between seeing your whole portfolio drop in half, with no distinction made between short and long-term money, and seeing stable returns in the safety bucket and dismal returns for longer-term investments. While 60% of SEI's investors in traditional allocations bailed or greatly reduced their equity exposure, the goals-based investors better realized that their near-term goals and financial obligations were unimpacted by the horrors of 2008, leading them to behave better.

Goals-based investing is a simple solution to a potentially devastating problem. The best plans crafted by the most elaborate algorithms focusing both on probabilistic market scenarios and identifying the optimal investment products mean nothing if the client panics when volatility spikes. GBI blissfully uncomplicates things by increasing the surface area of a portfolio, then labeling parts of it with a purpose.

By itself, catastrophizing with our money can lead to an incapacitating spiral of fear and shame. But if we pair our tendency to imagine the worst with a few small steps to take the worst case off the table, we can free our minds and our wallets to work toward bigger things and take appropriate risks.

Creating a safety bucket, simply by setting aside six to 24 months of cash or cash equivalents (depending on your personal level of anxiety), can reduce the intense fear that comes with market volatility or an individual money catastrophe like the loss of a job.

The peace of mind of knowing that daily expenses will be met allows you to shift your focus toward more constructive long-term thoughts and actions. That clearer mindset keeps the more distant plan moored and allows for the pursuit of bolder financial goals.

NOT BEING
DUMB BEATS
BEING BRILLIANT

T HE JANGLY GUITAR hook begins, and before you know it, you are tapping your feet. But then, the lyrics kick in, "Dumb ways to die, so many dumb ways to die."

Wait a minute, what?

This earworm, which you've likely encountered as part of some social media 'fail' compilation, has a storied past as one of the most important prevention campaigns of all time.

And it proved to be anything but a failure. The "Dumb Ways to Die" animated music video was conceived by Metro Trains in Melbourne, Australia to promote railway safety and reduce accidents on platforms. Rather than going the usual route of, say, hiring a spokesperson to pitch a serious-natured commercial, Metro Trains took a different route. They leveraged humor and creativity to effectively convey the message.

The ad was an animated music video featuring cute characters engaging in foolish and risky activities, such as standing too close to the tracks as a train approached. With its catchy tune, the video went viral and received nearly 200 million YouTube views. The video was no joke, though. High online engagement created a widespread buzz about the dangers of doing dumb stuff around trains. The campaign won multiple Grand Prix awards at the Cannes Lions International Festival of Creativity, among the most prestigious honors in the advertising field.

Despite not taking a conventional approach to public awareness, Metro Train found that there was a 21% reduction in railway mishaps within just six weeks of the ad's release. As a result, other municipalities adopted the strategy, though perhaps not earning the social reach of the Melbourne video. The coup de grâce of it all was that popularity was so high that it became a merchandising hit, which only further reinforced the safety message.

The financial services industry could use a little of that out-of-the-box marketing strategy. The typical ads about your money often include a couple sitting down with a dude in a suit going over some numbers, or a couple living up retirement on a sailboat. In addition to the sailboats (so many sailboats), mountains and compasses also make frequent appearances, all bathed in some non-offensive shade of blue.

Maybe such milquetoast approaches work for the affluent who are already on the right track, but so many of us are not even close and could use an irreverent jolt of the Dumb Ways to Die variety.

For example, not everyone who's offered an employer-sponsored retirement savings plan actually takes advantage of it. Of the 79% of Americans who have the option of investing in a workplace retirement plan, only 41% opt to participate. As such, less than one-in-three Americans is saving using a 401k.[176] And only about one-third of Americans diversify their portfolio.[177] Outside of investments, half of people don't have life insurance coverage.[178] Unsurprisingly then, just 33% of Americans have a written financial plan, with the rest claiming they do not have enough money to make it worthwhile, they lack the time for it, or they believe it's just too complicated.[179] Amid this apparent neglect for long-term wealth management, day trading and other risky money behaviors have been on the rise, spurred on in part by the Covid-19 meme stock mania.

Why does it seem that our financial priorities are so out of whack? And what can be done by industry practitioners to help fix this broken situation?

Maybe hiring a few marketing whiz-kids from Melbourne Metro Trains is a good idea. We need to flip the script from focusing on big-time success to honing in on getting the small things right.

You see, personal finance and investing are not about hitting home runs. It's not about being as savvy as the folksy Warren Buffett. Nor is it about taking advice from social media stars. Rather, it's about doing a few fundamental things right while avoiding major risks, then moving on to other parts of your life.

For an example of avoiding 'dumb ways to go broke', we can look no further than Warren Buffett's partner, the late Charlie Munger, who has this to say of the Berkshire approach that has made both men billionaires: "It is remarkable how much long-term advantage people like us have gotten by trying to be consistently not stupid, instead of trying to be very intelligent."

Sports get the point across, too. No game exemplifies the possible faults of unwise actions as well as tennis. Tennis is known as the "loser's game" in that successful players—be they Grand Slam champions or talented amateurs—know that the key to winning is just playing a clean game. While the winner's game involves skillful shots and thoughtful strategy, the loser's game emphasizes mistake minimization and not giving points away. It's said that pros win points while amateurs lose them.

Investing is the same way. Boring is beautiful. Going for the big score often results in a costly financial double fault.

For many families, step one in not being dumb is to protect against catastrophe. Holding the right amount of insurance, building an emergency fund, maintaining an estate plan, and even taking care of yourself health-wise can all help mitigate financial pitfalls.

When it comes to your investments, make it a point to save periodically, maybe through your retirement plan at work or in an IRA (or both). Once you have your investment train chugging along, be sure to diversify and plan for specific events, such as your children's college or your retirement.

If you have sufficient insurance, a cash safety net, and a basic portfolio, and still insist on picking individual stocks (despite everything you've read in this book), do so with a modest amount of your wealth—no more than 3% to 5% of your net worth. Maybe you'll hit a backhand winner, maybe you won't. Think of it like a cheat meal for your money.

If you're still daunted by some of these concepts, you are not alone. Most people, even those with a sack full of money, are not well-versed in how best to manage their finances. If that's you, first, you've taken the first step because your uncertainty shows that you've gotten beyond most people's overconfidence. Next, seek the help of a financial planner who can be your partner in aligning your money and values so that you can reach whatever goals you might have.

———

Much as the priority of any travel excursion is safety, the first goal of any financial plan must be avoiding catastrophe and error before moving on to higher-order considerations. But a combination of the illusion of control, confirmation bias, overconfidence, and a host of other behavioral blunders leads us in all the wrong directions.

Our biased human nature causes us to focus on sexy-but-inconsequential things like picking stocks, often neglecting more fundamental considerations like good advice, appropriate protection, adequate savings, and broad diversification. To use a car analogy, people would rather show off their engine than their airbags.

Don't fall for that mindset. Keep your finances simple so that you can avoid unhappy accidents.

HEALTH IS WEALTH

TWO YEARS AGO, I thought I was dying.

The pain began as a series of splitting headaches that would come on without warning and was so intense as to be debilitating. I couldn't eat, I couldn't work, I could only lie on my back in a dark room and hope for the headaches to go away.

Eager to resolve this issue, I started with the least intrusive possibility suggested by the internet: a toothache. I had never had a single cavity, let alone something more dramatic, but I went to my dentist to rule out a problem with my tooth. After a thorough examination, I was given a clean bill of dental health and was turned back into the world with no answers and a series of scarier options to consider.

Over the next few months, I visited every conceivable type of doctor trying to find the source of the pain that alternated between being non-existent and crippling. I visited an ear-nose-and-throat specialist, neurologist, psychiatrist, and got a CT scan.

Nothing.

I tried homeopathic treatments, oxygen therapy, meditation, and dietary changes.

Nothing.

I was six months into a life of blinding pain that would come on without warning or seeming cause, when one night the agony became so intense that I went to the emergency room. On the drive there, I finally broke down, sobbing for fear that I would be permanently broken by some mysterious ailment that I was powerless to diagnose or treat.

A night in the ER and a series of further tests yielded no further light and I found myself at one of the lowest points of my life. It is no exaggeration to say that I would have given you every dollar I had at that moment if you could have shown me the source of my pain and offered me some comfort.

A few days later, I was having lunch at a client event in Atlanta when my face began to swell dramatically. Excusing myself to the bathroom, I noticed that my gums were the source of the inflammation and that something was clearly wrong with my tooth, the original suspect in this half-year-long battle with suffering. Later that day, a now deeply cracked tooth was pulled and the pain immediately subsided, never to return.

I am someone who likes money. I write about it, I talk about it, I study it for a living, and I think about it more than I should. But during those months when my health was in question, money was the furthest thing from my mind, and my only financial thought was if and how I could use my money to buy myself better health. The fact is, there is no true wealth without health, and gains we make to improve our physical, mental, and psychological well-being tend to better our financial lives, and vice versa.

The wallet-body connection is a very real phenomenon. While I was fortunate to have the financial resources to seek cures for my mysterious condition, so many individuals and families struggle just to meet daily living expenses. That constant stress weighs heavily—financial stressors have been found to directly correlate with poor physical and mental well-being. Research published in

Social Science & Medicine found that debt-related financial distress increases the odds of developing depression by 51%.[180]

Furthermore, money stress can manifest in physical symptoms, such as insomnia, migraines, compromised immune systems, digestive issues, and more. Even if you don't have something physically bothering you due to financial woes, you might find that when an unexpected bill arrives, you don't reach for your checkbook to take care of the issue, rather you grab a carton of ice cream as a coping mechanism.

Worry is indeed a major issue in today's culture—with worldwide levels of anxiety reaching record highs during and after the Covid-19 pandemic. Sixty percent of Americans report feeling anxious about their financial status, with younger generations more likely to feel worry, according to a 2023 Mind of Money survey by Capital One.[181]

So, whether you face a crippling condition or experience a bit of pecuniary panic, there's often an interplay between health and wealth.

But let's follow Charlie Munger's advice for a moment and "invert, always invert." Just as financial anxiety can lead to physical problems, health issues can likewise result in a step-up in money stress. And, as was my case, physical debilitation got in the way of work. Maybe you have experienced something similar and have lost out on a paycheck or had your career progress halted for a time.

Workers burdened by financial worries are more susceptible to developing various health problems, including heart disease, diabetes, migraines, sleep problems, chronic pain, and more. These conditions often result in costly medical bills, perpetuating financial worry and instability. Evidence shows that people with higher financial difficulties were more likely to experience some of these bad health outcomes.[182]

The BrightPlan 2023 Wellness Barometer Survey found that people lose about one day of work per week due to financial stress. The survey also revealed that a significant portion of respondents (72%) occasionally miss out on social engagements—such as attending weddings or going out with friends for dinner and drinks—due to financial constraints.[183] These are sobering stats, and they should serve to underscore the importance of taking advantage of all your available resources, such as wellness plans through your employer or simply dedicating time for mental rejuvenation and physical fitness.

Bigger picture, our economy faces long-term risks if we continue to neglect our collective health. A 2018 report by insurance services firm Willis Towers Watson examined the correlation between employees' financial concerns and work performance. Among individuals struggling financially, there's 41% more work time lost compared to their peers not claiming money stress. Moreover, they exhibited an estimated 27% decrease in productivity compared to the non-stressed group.[184] At the aggregate level, financial stress is estimated to cost U.S. employers upwards of $200 billion annually.

Are we destined for a life of constant money stress and never-ending medical bills?

Not necessarily. Nancy Cook, employee assistance counselor at Purdue University's Center for Healthy Living, suggests we take a close look at our individual financial situation and then take proactive steps to reach out for help. We can also train our brains to be more rational about money.

Just as Cook suggests getting real with your budget is key, acknowledging the emotional component of the health-wealth connection is an important initial step. You can then make rational decisions to better your financial situation. Those actions might include investing more for long-term goals, building an emergency fund, and dedicating a portion of your budget to health and wellness.

Consider this incentive: There's evidence that regular exercise can positively impact your salary. According to a study conducted by economist Vasilios Kosteas from Cleveland State University, frequent exercise can potentially result in up to a 10% increase in pay.[185]

Also, do this for me: Picture yourself decades down the line. Yes, it may seem distant and vague, but visualizing your future self can help you prioritize things today—your daily routine, your diet, trips you want to embark on, and people you want to get closer to. All of those factors impact your body, and as described above, your financial condition.

One of my favorite podcast guests of the last few years has been Dr. Michael Finke. Or should I say, "Dr. Dr." Michael Finke because he has not one, but two, Ph.D.s. Michael is a nationally renowned researcher with a focus on the value of financial advice, financial planning regulation, investments, and individual investor behavior. But his first Ph.D. was actually in the world of diet and exercise, where he quite by accident discovered an incredibly strong relationship between those who were physically fit and those who had great saving and investing behavior.

Who knew that a regular workout could also beef up your bank account?

There is an inextricable link between health and wealth, one that I experienced firsthand. Physical and mental health challenges can lead to financial stress (and vice versa), which hinders career progress and may set us back on our path to financial independence. We must all utilize available resources, such as wellness plans and self-care practices, to improve both health and financial stability. Focusing on one and not the other is tantamount to ignoring both.

YOUR MONEY,
YOUR VOTE

THE WAY YOU spend your money is a vote for the kind of world you want.

As an Alabamian, I have long marveled at the stories of civil rights leaders who spearheaded vital transformations in my Sweet Home. Since I'm also a financial history enthusiast, I'm especially interested in how Southern and other leaders throughout time have used economic means to bring about social change.

The Montgomery Bus Boycott, sparked by Rosa Parks' refusal to cede her seat, used both personal bravery and economic pressures to catalyze change.

Often first encountered by students in high school social studies classes as a poignant moment in the civil rights movement, the boycott's economic backstory is frequently overlooked.

In December 1955, Parks was arrested in Montgomery for violating segregation laws. A humble seamstress, with no ill intentions, her actions without conflict ignited a firestorm against racial discrimination.

African American community leaders immediately voted with their feet and wallets. Jo Ann Robinson and a young minister named Martin Luther King Jr. organized a citywide boycott of the

Montgomery bus system to challenge segregationist policies on public transit. The boycott was effective since African Americans constituted about 75% of the city's bus ridership. Many of them banded together, relying on carpooling, African American-owned taxis, or simply walking.

With unwavering determination and peaceful resolve, their boycott hit the Montgomery City Lines' coffers hard. Revenue plummeted as Dr. King, among other community leaders, pursued legal challenges to the constitutionality of segregated public transportation.

Following a federal lawsuit, arguing that the city's actions violated the Fourteenth Amendment's Equal Protection Clause, the Supreme Court declared racial segregation on public buses was unconstitutional. The Court's landmark ruling forced the integration of the Montgomery bus system, putting a successful end to the boycott. The reverberations of this victory were felt nationwide, as the Montgomery Bus Boycott inspired other nonviolent protests and furthered the momentum of the civil rights movement.

Voting with your budget has profound power. Citizens of Montgomery leveraged their collective economic influence and dealt a severe financial blow to the city's bus operator in an effort to bring about positive social change. The boycott stands as a testament to the potential of consumer actions to pave the way for progress.

And it's not the only instance of how economics has been a tool to promote the general welfare of all people. The Stamp Act and subsequent Boston Tea Party during the American colonial period is another example.

The British Parliament passed the Stamp Act in 1765 to help pay for British soldiers stationed in the colonies during the Seven Years' War. The Act mandated that colonists pay a tax, represented by a stamp, on things ranging from important documents to playing cards. Seen as taxation without representation, the colonists' rebellion came in the form of a refusal to purchase or import taxed items. This initial act of defiance foreshadowed further events to come.

Eight years later, one of the most iconic boycotts of all unfolded. In response to the British government's Tea Act, which granted a monopoly over the tea trade to the British East India Company, American colonists united in resolute opposition to British tea. Emotions reached a boiling point, culminating in the famous Boston Tea Party.

American history is rooted in the power of money, but we are not alone in using economic connectedness to drive progressive social reform.

Beyond our borders, Mahatma Gandhi's leadership during India's quest for independence provides further evidence of the transformative impact financial crusades can have. Through his Khadi Movement, Gandhi orchestrated boycotts of British textiles and encouraged his compatriots to opt for homespun clothing as a symbol of independence. More impressive still, he embarked on a 240-mile march to the Arabian Sea to produce salt from seawater in defiance of the British monopoly on salt production and high tariffs. The indomitable spirit of the Indian people and their commitment to achieving independence was on clear display.

Then during apartheid in South Africa, when racial segregation and discrimination were systematically enforced, divestment campaigns gained traction as a means to exert economic pressure on the ruling body. By disrupting economic stability, citizens sought to raise awareness about ongoing injustices. On top of that, sports boycotts on the international stage emerged as a formidable method to challenge the apartheid system. Rugby and cricket matches were seen as a duel between activists and the oppressive regime. The boycotts served to undermine the power of those in control and showcased global solidarity against racial oppression.

It can be easy to look at the grand, sweeping economic actions that led to progress from Birmingham to Cape Town and feel as though our actions don't matter much. But the reality is that every dollar you spend is a powerful vote for the kind of world in which you want to live.

In the U.S., we have the privilege of voting for a new president every four years. In Mexico, it occurs every six years, and in France, elections take place every seven years. However often it happens where you live (it's three to five years in most countries), you likely do the time-consuming work of getting to know the various candidates, exploring their policies, and then casting a vote for the candidate who best embodies your most deeply held convictions. But each day, we encounter myriad chances to do the very same thing with our spending choices—an opportunity that most of us let slip by with little thought.

Here's an easy framework you can put to work to align your spending with your values. Maybe you won't change the world as Rosa Parks did, but by taking small financial steps, you can move closer to living in the world you wish to see.

- **Realize that you're voting**: When you spend, you are voting—whether you know it or not. I don't think people fully understand this. Rather, we tend to click 'add to cart' without giving it much thought. But each buy has an impact.
- **Review your spending habits**: Take a closer look at where your money flows each month. Reflect on whether your financial choices align with your values and the kind of world you aspire to support.
- **Educate yourself**: You don't need to be a news junkie, but at least stay informed about the practices, policies, and values of the brands you buy.

- **Support firms that share your worldview**: Become a customer of businesses that actively promote and embody the causes you care about, whether it is upholding family values, supporting women, equitable business practices, or kindness to animals.
- **Shop local**: Consider the benefits of supporting nearby businesses, as money spent within your community tends to endure and offers an upside to your locale, versus buying from a multinational corporation. According to Fundera by NerdWallet, small companies generate $68 of local economic benefit for every $100 spent.[186] Why not buy from a mom-and-pop shop down the street and help out your neighbors at the same time?
- **Vote your shares**: Investors should consider exercising shareholder power by putting dollars to work in public companies that align with their values. Proxy voting and additional engagement put the power in shareholders' hands.

In a very real sense, it is up to you and me to be the heart and soul of capitalism. Capitalism, when applied appropriately, possesses immense power for good; truly, no system has done more to lift people from poverty. However, in another respect, capitalism is amoral, responding solely to the whims of you and me, its stewards, and captains. Sustainable packaging, Fair Trade-certified products, organic food, cruelty-free cosmetics, electric vehicles—each of these is nothing more than the market's response to the voice of the consumer. Though voter turnout in the U.S. is typically around 60%, each of us votes every day in a manner that is just as powerful, yet often unheralded.

You can choose to vote consciously with your money or unconsciously, but the reality is that we all vote. Exercise this power with open eyes.

A GOOD FINANCIAL PLAN LEAVES ROOM FOR GROWTH

W HAT HAPPENS WHEN someone commands you not to do something? Well, if you're like me, it makes you want to try it that much more. Whether it's a child and a hot stove, a teenager and forbidden love, or a dieter and a cookie, nothing makes us want something like knowing we can't have it.

I first read *The Catcher in the Rye* in middle school, precisely because some adults in my life had warned me against the book. The text piqued my interest for its controversial reputation, even being banned in some circles and having loose connections with dangerous men.

For me, a chubby, poofy-haired kid with a penchant for wearing pastel polos, the hope was that perhaps some of that menacing aura would rub off. Many years later, I'm no more dangerous, but I do have a deeper understanding of one of the psychological drivers of the book—a tendency psychologists refer to as the end of history illusion.

The novel's protagonist, Holden Caulfield, is a teenager battling some of the life challenges I faced at the same age. He struggled to pin down a confident identity as he transitioned into adulthood. Caulfield found himself longing for the past, feeling nostalgia for years gone by and seeking meaning during his adolescence.

His perspective is a prime example of the end of history illusion. He sees himself as fully formed with little growth ahead and no catalysts to bring about a renewed and different sense of self. Consumed by the belief that most of life's significant moments had come and gone, he found himself detached from the present and with a lack of hope for the future.

The end of history illusion is a cognitive bias in which people sometimes see the current version of themselves as enduring, but in a bad way. They regard their personal development and growth as waning, leading them to miss out on opportunities for self-improvement.

In the book, Caulfield fixates on childhood memories—their innocence, authenticity, and unfettered relationships. When looking at his years ahead, there's angst and worry as he perceives the world as being filled with disingenuous people and hypocrisy at every turn. That uncomfortable internal status and outside view cause him to withdraw and resist the inevitable maturity that comes with aging into adulthood.

But as the story unfolds, Caulfield experiences situations of self-reflection and introspection to challenge his limiting beliefs. Along the way, he encounters various characters and grapples with his own internal issues. Caulfield gradually recognizes that personal growth is not a one-and-done adolescent event. Changes are always happening, and they are to be embraced.

The Catcher in the Rye reminds readers that life is a journey of change and development. We are always learning new things, taking in memorable experiences, and influencing others around us—often unknowingly. Viewing oneself as stagnant harms us not just in the moment but also over the years and decades to come.

I saw this in my own life recently as I dug up some old journals from a time when I served a two-year mission for my church in the Philippines. I visibly cringed as I revisited my own thoughts and feelings from that time. Ashamed of my immaturity and wincing at my lack of perspective, I quickly re-shelved the dusty tomes, thinking to myself, "Thank goodness I'm nothing like that anymore."

What does Holden Caulfield have to do with your financial plan?

Well, you, like Caulfield, are prone to thinking that your best days are behind you and that you've grown all you're going to grow. In short, you believe that who you are today is all you will ever be.

But that attitude sells you short. The end of history illusion dismisses the very real (and very positive!) fact that you will continue to evolve and mature and, as a result, leads you to set financial decisions in stone that may crumble along life's rocky path.

The end of history illusion says that we can read journals from 20 years ago and readily articulate how little we have in common with that person, but it blinds us to the undeniable truth that our 20-years-from-now selves will be every bit as unrecognizable.

What this requires of us financially is to balance preparation with flexibility, understanding that we need a plan to guide us and that the plan should be a living document that is amenable to growth and change.

Alfred Korzybski put it well: "The map is not the territory." The philosopher and scientist's turn of phrase conveys that people tend to conflate models of reality with reality itself, then run into danger from their too-literal adherence to a 'map'. The expression serves as a reminder that our mental constructs are often too restrictive and may not capture the richness and nuances of the present and future. General guidelines and guardrails are helpful, but there must be a degree of flexibility and even creativity built in.

We see this trap in financial planning all the time. Here are just a few general money principles that are all too often interpreted more as gospel rather than mendable:

- **The 4% rule**: Also known as the Safe Withdrawal Rate in retirement, this rule of thumb suggests that a retiree can withdraw 4% of their portfolio annually without a significant risk of running out of savings over a 30-year period. While studies show it can work, strictly following the 4% rule can result in financial peril due to both an individual's circumstances changing and market factors.
- **The 10% annualized equity returns rule**: From 1928 through 2022, the S&P 500 had a compounded annual growth rate of 9.7%, according to data from NYU Stern.[187] Long-term averages are useful, but they shouldn't be assumed going forward. What's more, the range of yearly returns is massive, from −44% to +53%, so any single year can venture far from the 10% long-term norm. Discounting that risk puts financial plans in jeopardy.
- **The retire at 65 rule**: Just simply the notion of retirement is something new. As recently as 100 years ago, we basically worked until we croaked. Then, when Social Security was launched in 1935, the retirement age was set at 65 as most people didn't even make it that long.[188] Back then, women aged to 62 while the typical man died at 58. Today, outliving your money is a major risk if you assume you can hang 'em up at 65 without a significant investment portfolio. Today's kids may even live to 100 and beyond.[189]

All of these are good rules of thumb, but none of them are immutable Laws of the Universe and we should never confuse finance with physics. George Box's admonition, "All models are wrong, but some are useful," is a perfect fit for planning your financial life. Operating without a plan leads to chaos and lack of coordination, and studies suggest that simply having a living, breathing financial plan results in better financial outcomes and happiness.

A 2021 Charles Schwab survey found that just 33% of Americans have a written financial plan, and among those, 65% reported feeling financially stable, compared to just 40% of those without a plan.[190] Maybe more striking, 54% of the planning group felt "very confident" about achieving their financial goals, compared with only 18% of non-planners feeling that same degree of assurance.

But even as you chart the course of your financial journey, be sure to maintain appropriate room for growth and change. Heraclitus' ageless quote, "No man ever steps in the same river twice, for it's not the same river and he's not the same man," is as true of your money as it is of your life.

BEING RICH
REQUIRES BEING
WEIRD

NOBODY LIKES TO be average. As a young psychologist giving IQ assessments to children, the hardest news for me to deliver to parents was that a child's IQ was in the normal range.

High IQ? Brilliant! I knew my little snookums was a genius. Low IQ? This makes sense, we've been having trouble at school and now we know where to start. But average IQ? Nobody wanted that news.

It turns out that what's true of suburban parents is also true of your ability to create and grow your wealth—you don't want to be average. In fact, you want to be a little weird.

Olympic Games aficionados may recall one innovation that, at the time, was truly in the *that looks really weird* category. The so-called Fosbury Flop was met with skeptical eyes early on, but its innovator, Dick Fosbury, struck gold with it.

_____

High jumping is an Olympic sporting event in which competitors attempt to leap as high as possible over a bar.

Pretty simple, right?

Up until the Fosbury Flop, jumpers used the conventional 'straddle' or 'scissors' method. That approach involved the jumper facing the bar, then straddling their legs over it, using their upper body to clear the bar. For decades, that was the normal strategy. Nobody questioned it.

Fosbury, determined to improve his stature in high jumping, came up with a better way. Rather than facing the bar, he turned his back to it while in flight, arching his body in such a way that looked like an odd somersault in the air. While it garnered cockeyed looks at the time, and even ridicule from his competitors, it soon drew awe.

As the 1968 Olympics in Mexico City neared, Fosbury was at home practicing for hours and days on end, all while the rest of the high jumping world was doing the same old thing. At the games, he showcased his prowess (and weirdness). Clearing the bar at 2.24 meters (more than 7 feet), he set a new world record, earning him the gold medal.

The world of high jumping was forever changed. Elite athletes were forced to upend their methods, while up-and-comers were taught a new way of doing things by some of the same coaches who had only recently mocked Fosbury. Leap ahead to today, and we see high jumpers doing the Fosbury Flop at the Olympics every four years.

The story of the Fosbury Flop makes total sense in retrospect to those familiar with the sport. At the time, though, few in high jumping would have dared to go against the herd.

Thinking differently—and especially acting differently—are uncomfortable. Humans are tribal. We are desperate to be part of a crowd and to fit in. While being communal serves us well to build social connections, it is also one of the greatest dangers to our wealth-building potential.

The typical person consumes too much, is reliant on debt, and falls victim to haphazard investing tendencies. That's what passes for normal in the world of personal finance. To do better with your money, you must sometimes go with the Fosbury Flop mindset. Just as Dick countered the conventional technique, you have to think differently than the crowd. It may be painful initially, but that is often the first step to great progress.

According to data from the Federal Reserve Bank of New York, Americans hold nearly $1 trillion in credit card debt as of the first quarter of 2023—the highest balance since the NY Fed began tracking it in 1999. If that's normal, then you should embrace the desire to be weird. While friends, family, and those obnoxious neighbors of yours show off their sports cars, flashy toys, and new boats, it's natural to feel like you are owed a little something, too.

But those luxuries, especially the big-ticket items, should only come after you have laid the groundwork for sound saving and investing strategies. Going for broke by constantly swiping a credit card is not going to improve your financial stature. The Fosbury Flop way of thinking would be to focus on your future self, not your acquaintances and all their new toys.

What else is weird?

Budgeting.

While only financial nerds enjoy messing with spreadsheets and diving into apps to track income and expenses, it's sometimes the medicine we must swallow to get on the right footing with our money. A 2018 study found that 35% of respondents simply forgot to make a credit card payment. Just tracking your cash inflows and outflows can set you on a better financial course.[191]

The innate feeling to be tribal is seen in the investment world, too. As Ben Carlson related in *A Wealth of Common Sense*, "A study performed by the Federal Reserve... looked at mutual fund inflows and outflows over nearly 30 years from 1984 to 2012. Predictably, they found that most investors poured money into the markets after large gains and pulled money out after sustaining losses—a buy high, sell low debacle of a strategy."

We can stand on the sidelines mocking that subpar method of buying only after markets have rallied, but it's a trap we can all so easily fall prey to.

Going against the grain is actually easier than you think in this instance. Rather than trying to time the market, buying only at the lows and selling when you think stocks have gone too high, just take a simple approach. A regular investing plan like buying every two weeks or every month is all that's necessary to beat most investors. While it's not a competition, you will be winning if you just avoid letting the booms and busts of stocks disrupt your investing routine.

Whether it is managing debt, budgeting, or investing, what most people do with their money isn't exactly the best.

You are wired to fit in—but creating a rich life will require you to stand apart from the crowd. Dick Fosbury proved that long-term success can mean short-term pain and social derision, and it requires bravery to be willing to go down the road less traveled.

In markets, being right in any meaningful way requires bravery to hold a different opinion and conviction that you are right when others are doing it wrong. Thousands of books, authored by some of the most genius financial minds, have been written about how to be right when allocating assets and making investment decisions, but bravery, boldness, and even embracing the weird are understudied and underutilized. Here's to you, you weirdo.

FINANCE IS A
HUMANITY

Money is often viewed as black and white, Xs and Os, numbers on a page that have little to teach us. But since money touches every part of our lives and the world, the study of money ends up being the study of both people and planet.

For evidence of this, look no further than what the characters at the heart of *The Big Short* did to predict a housing market crash and stock market turmoil during the Great Financial Crisis.

Sure, like thousands of other Wall Street stock-pickers and portfolio managers, they parsed company financial statements and dug into all the key economic data points. But they also took some odd and extreme measures to gauge the world around them. The protagonists—Michael Burry, Mark Baum, and Steve Eisman—did everything from visiting strip clubs and home foreclosure auctions to speak with local homeowners to get a sense of the landscape. That's, um, quite an education.

These famed shortsellers know that finance is part art, part science, and that it's impossible to understand the numbers without grokking the human stories that sit just below the surface. Speak with most financial advisors and they will likely vouch for that, with many telling me that they wish they had earned a degree in psychology, instead of one more ostensibly financial. The same concept goes for your financial life; as you learn more about money, you'll learn more about the world.

Have you ever met with a well-intended wealth manager whom you paid to craft a sound financial plan? Were you delivered a fancy-looking binder chock full of percentages and pie charts? A heavy and dusty tome that was never revisited? This sort of well-intended overwhelm was standard practice for years, but often left clients more confused than they began.

But the advisory industry is coming around to the notion that a perfect financial plan means nothing if the human side of money and the why of wealth aren't put front and center. That's good news. It is also something everyday investors should embrace.

I'm not suggesting you gauge the state of the macro environment by taking your family to a gentlemen's club (as *The Big Short* might suggest), but you can use finance to discover the world in ways you perhaps had not thought of. Get out there and go experience something new.

Something new could be as easy as diving into a book genre you haven't exposed yourself to before. You'll be more cultured just by reading past the cover. According to a 2021 report by Pew Research, 23% of Americans had not read a book over the past year (and people had plenty of spare time back then, as I recall).[192] Another reality underscoring most folks' lack of cultural exposure: The average American lives just 18 miles from their mom, according to an Upshot analysis of data from the Health and Retirement Study.[193]

Here's where finance can be your best companion to discovering new adventures and widening your horizons.

It's different from other disciplines. Learning its ropes means grasping how so many aspects of life interact. Financial expert

Jared Dillian highlights that working in finance equips you with an understanding of what makes the world go around. People in finance can piece together the individual data points of why, say, used car prices surged. Or what caused a dozen eggs to soar to $5 at the grocery store. Through studying markets, a financier becomes conversant in supply chains, global epidemics, geopolitics, trade issues, and even just people's vibes. Dillian asserts that, "A kid from Staten Island can get hired and within a few years, acquire enough sophistication to carry on an intelligent conversation with most world leaders."

Studying money is more than just examining dollars and cents. Let's go back to the pandemic (actually, please, let's not do that). But just recall all the financial hoopla that went on from 2020 through 2021. Finance and investing quickly turned mainstream. So-called *meme stocks* and cryptocurrencies were the talk of social media, and among socially distanced moms and dads at birthday parties. A survey from Ally Financial found that two-in-five Americans traded a meme stock back then, including 66% of millennials.[194] Human psychology and the state of daily living drew otherwise uninterested people to learn about investing.

We were all cooped up at home, Uncle Sam deposited a bunch of cash in our bank accounts, trading apps had just taken off, and FOMO (along with a few strains of Covid-19) was in the air. The human side of meme stock mania fascinated both professionals and non-numbers people alike. Excess savings, the availability of free-trading platforms, boredom, and a lack of other entertainment (many sports were shut down) drove individuals to try their luck at day trading. The same root cause analysis and dot-connecting are done with less sexy topics like currency devaluation and wholesale trade trends. But no matter the instance, finance insights and knowledge deepen comprehension of our immediate and distant surroundings.

So, I encourage you to diversify. I'm not talking about shifting your asset allocation, or selling your stock in your employer. What I am saying is that you can take a page from Finance 101 and challenge yourself to do something different. Shake up your routine, go to unfamiliar places, and expose yourself to ideas contrary to what you believe. Do it on a daily, weekly, monthly, and yearly basis.

Here's how you can push yourself beyond your usual orbit:

- **Daily**: Listen to a new podcast or bring up a new conversation subject with a friend or colleague.
- **Weekly**: Go to a local theater to catch a show outside of your usual interests, or try a new Friday lunch spot.
- **Monthly**: Read a book. Any book. Apparently most of us are terrible at this. Preferably, make it something out of your norm. Or volunteer a few hours for a cause near to your heart.
- **Yearly**: Embark on a trip to a new spot and take in a different culture, then set financial goals upon reflection on the year that was.

Money touches every part of our lives and every part of our world. It is intertwined with our society, history, and communal ideologies. While the study and pursuit of finance is often uninspiring and predictable at its most basic level, if we look beyond the surface and examine everything that money impacts, it can provide valuable insights into our shared world and the people within it.

Finance, framed as a humanity, not a science, opens gateways to new ideas and experiences that can change us and help us become better versions of ourselves.

YOU ARE NOT
YOUR THINGS

I T's PART OF the human condition that we desire more. We are wired to always want something bigger and better, new and improved. And for better and worse, it's our acquisitive nature that takes free-market economies around the world to new heights.

Whether it's an innovative start-up disrupting an industry with a revolutionary gadget, or just a personal craving for, say, a luxurious new robe, there's nothing wrong with a dash of ambition and aspiration. For consumers like you and me, though, danger lurks when we fail to temper our natural inclination to accumulate and upgrade rather than simplify and eliminate.

This tendency is known as the Diderot Effect, a condition in which one seemingly innocuous purchase leads us down a rabbit hole of ultra-consumerism.

Denis Diderot was a famous 18th-century French philosopher, and co-founder and writer of the *Encyclopédie*. By all accounts, he was living a content life without much in the way of material possessions. That all changed when Diderot found himself light on cash to fund a proper dowry for his daughter's marriage. Catherine the Great heard of his money troubles and offered to buy his library for £1,000—about $60,000 today. With that cash injection, Diderot was able to fund the dowry, splash out on lavish items for the wedding, and also buy an item or two that he fancied for himself.

Diderot treated himself to a scarlet robe. The flashy garment stood out in his wardrobe and so, naturally, he felt compelled to upgrade his other possessions to match the grandeur of this impressive robe. Thus began his trip on the hamster wheel of materialism. Diderot quipped, "no more coordination, no more unity, no more beauty." The only solution, in his mind, was to procure more possessions that could equal the robe's beauty.

After a series of lavish purchases, his home was chock full of sculptures and exquisite furniture. The philosopher succumbed to the same consumer trap that plagues us today. One money splurge begets another, then another, and we continue on the hamster wheel, much to the delight of countless corporate marketing departments.

The Diderot Effect may fill your home and your life with luxury, but it can rob your bank account. It's fine to have a goal to buy a new car, keep up with fashion trends, or even have high-end appliances, but you run a personal finance foul when your stuff accumulates while your happiness stagnates.

Sometimes it takes a little Marie Kondo to simplify your life and boost contentment.

One tip is for every one item you acquire, get rid of (or donate) another—the *buy one, give one* technique. Another tip is to reduce your exposure to triggers. As author James Clear points out, nearly every habit is initiated by a trigger, so unsubscribing to emails, avoiding budget-draining malls, and limiting time on certain shopping websites can help mitigate the Diderot Effect. The goal is to enjoy life and ensure a sound financial tomorrow.

The Diderot Effect is portrayed in modern culture in Chuck Palahniuk's *Fight Club*. It tells the tale of a man leading a regular life, working a soul-crushing job, and getting his dopamine hits through material things. Before long, the Narrator becomes a slave to his possessions, equating what he owns with his self-worth. The world of Fight Club, an underground rebellion group of violent dudes, impresses on him that the culture of consumerism is superficial and harmful.

Perhaps the story's most well-known tagline, "the things you own end up owning you," is an apt description of our consumer culture today. It's as if we look to possessions to fill some void in us. A void that material wealth can never fully and finally satisfy. Rather, 'the things' all too often dictate our actions and control our thoughts at the expense of freedom and peace.

Fight Club urges us to counter our consumer-driven society by discovering fulfillment through human connections and personal growth rather than obsessively turning to objects for some kind of validation. The book and movie not only describe the cycle of consumption precipitated by a big purchase but also speak to the very human tendency to equate what we own with who we are.

Part of what drives our hunger for more is that the mind makes little distinction between *possessing* and *being*, at least in the anticipatory stages of consumption. The Having-Being Fallacy tells us that by owning an object, we become what it embodies. So, in a very real sense, we think that by buying that Tag Heuer Monaco, we will literally become effortlessly cool like Steve McQueen. Were this true, it would be a remarkable shortcut to, you know, having a personality and being worth talking to. However, the having-being connection proves to be illusory in the long run, no matter how compelling it may seem in the throes of pre-purchase longing.

The Narrator in *Fight Club* (played in the movie by Edward Norton) remarks to Tyler Durden (played by Brad Pitt) that his life was almost complete before he lost all his material things in a fire. He goes on to enumerate how he had assembled a nice stereo system, a set of perfectly imperfect dishware, a respectable wardrobe, and a few more trappings of middle-class success. In response, Durden tries to sever this having-being fallacy with one of his best lines:

> You are not your job, you're not how much money you have in the bank. You are not the car you drive. You're not the contents of your wallet. You are not your... khakis.

————————

From real-life examples, like Diderot and Howard Hughes, to fictional embodiments like The Narrator, we see that humankind is prone to taking shortcuts on the rocky road of self-creation, detouring us toward consumerism. This would be bad enough on its own, of course, but the combination of the Having-Being Fallacy and the Diderot Effect mean that not only do we think that we are our khakis but also that our khakis can set in motion a series of subsequent purchases in a fruitless effort to try to hang on to this veneer of self.

Breaking free of these two intertwined cycles means asking ourselves a few hard questions:

- Am I buying this because of what I feel it conveys about my identity?
- Is there a more enduring way of becoming the person I aspire to be that doesn't require consumerism?
- What additional items will this purchase precipitate?

————————

I write all of this from a place of absolute hypocrisy—my home is littered with items of interest. I have a closet full of Jordans but a vertical that's not going to break any combine records, a baseball card collection that cheaply masks my inability to hit a curve ball, and a library that is equal parts knowledge repository and pretentious conversation starter for visitors to the house.

It's unlikely that any of us will ever totally overcome the desire to be a little more 'X' if only we could purchase 'Y'. And I'm not saying we should eschew all material items, buy a couple of goats and some chickens, and live off-grid.

However, by increasing our understanding of the dual mirages of the Having-Being Fallacy and the Diderot Effect, we can devote a little more time toward true fulfillment and a little less time shopping for the thing that we believe will complete us.

IMAGINING THE WORST CAN BE FOR THE BEST

"FORMULATE AND STAMP indelibly on your mind a mental picture of yourself as succeeding. Hold this picture tenaciously. Never permit it to fade. Your mind will seek to develop the picture… Do not build up obstacles in your imagination."

The homespun optimism of Norman Vincent Peale's *The Power of Positive Thinking* has a simple logic that has led it to sell over five million copies and be translated into 40 languages. One of those copies was given to me by my Nana in college, presumably her response to the moodier French existentialism that was captivating my thoughts at the time.

Peale's success owes to painting a picture of a world filled with optimism and belief, and it's an appealing vision to be sure. But as you've seen throughout this book, there are times when doing the exact opposite of what seems sensible can have a sense of its own. All of which leads me to ask:

Are there times when imagining the worst can be for the best?

Negative visualization was a practice invented by the Stoics thousands of years ago. They called it the premeditation of evils, or *Premeditatio Malorum*. Writers and philosophers like Marcus Aurelius and Seneca would detail everything that could lead to disaster. Back then, one bad move on a journey through the woods or on the high seas could result in death. And while most of us are blissfully immune to fatal sea voyages these days, weighing what could go wrong with your money can still have a salutary effect on your ability to reach financial freedom.

The underlying idea is that imagining the worst that could happen actually robs fear of its power. By checking all your blind spots ahead of time, you inherently build backup plans in the event there are bumps in your financial journey.

Here's a way to grasp the power of negative visualization in today's context: Picture yourself in a meeting at work. The boss outlines a sales strategy that's supposedly sure to increase business in the next quarter. You're skeptical. You read the room, and so are others. In your mind, you run through all the possible flaws in what you hear.

The worst thing that can happen is if nobody suggests what could go wrong with the boss's idea. Running through possible— maybe likely—pitfalls, in effect, surrounds the proposed strategy with risk management. This approach of *negative* thinking is emerging as an imperative box to check in boardrooms across the world. It's proven to increase the chance of identifying reasons for future failure by 30%.

For you as an investor, negative visualization helps to understand financial risk and the problems that come with it. As setbacks then happen, not only will you feel prepared, but you might even sense gratitude. It's like you'll thank your younger self for looking at the full scope, not just the optimistic angle. That gratitude then emboldens you to continue on the road to financial freedom.

Happiness garnered from strictly thinking about the bright side is often fleeting, but planning based on probabilistic worst-case scenarios generates enduring peace of mind.

The modern solution to the ancient art of premeditation is what social scientists refer to as a 'pre-mortem', a sort of negative visualization checklist. It builds wiggle room into any plan—from the risk of taking a shower in a slippery bathtub, to saving for retirement in a volatile market. This head-on approach to inevitable problems provides flexibility and nimbleness.

While post-mortems analyze the cause of what went wrong, a pre-mortem examines the range of negative outcomes. Psychologists assert that this process safeguards against potential points of failure.

Back to our corporate meeting room example—after the team had been briefed on the plan, the boss should have then asked everyone to write down all the reasons they could think of for the hypothetical failure of that plan. Next, each team member mentions their reasons until all are heard. Afterward, a complete list of weaknesses and threats to the plan are known and worked into the strategy.

Applying the logic of the boardroom to your personal finances, here are some steps you can take that embrace the same concept:

1. *Define financial goals meaningful to you*: Put pen to paper to list money's purposes in your life. "Retirement for my spouse and me," "Provide my children with a college education," or something less deep such as, "Complete my baseball card collection."

2. *Imagine, even embrace, failure*: Here's where you have to crawl in the mud a bit—it's the essence of a pre-mortem. Envision scenarios where money matters go awry. Ask yourself, "If I haven't met one of these goals by XYZ timeframe, what is the likely reason?" A job loss, a major unexpected bill, or just a poor stretch in the stock market could all result in falling short of your financial objectives.

3. *Determine potential causes*: For each point of failure, identify the reason. There were likely a range of factors. Overspending, neglecting to build and maintain an emergency fund, failing to update insurance policies as life changes, or banking on a never-ending bull market are all possible pitfalls.

4. *Weigh the risks*: Assess the likelihood and probability of each cause and bring it back to reality. Consider which potential potholes you are most likely to encounter, and which would have the biggest negative impact on your financial goals.

5. *Mitigate the risks*: It's time for action. Develop strategies to reduce both the chance of those risks and their impact should any occur. Reaching out to a financial advisor may help in this process. Build that emergency fund, ensure your portfolio is diversified, refresh your insurance coverage, and strive to build your professional skills.

6. *Live it*: Putting pre-mortem action items into practice requires new money habits and maybe even reconsidering old approaches. While not easy, lifestyle changes may be necessary.

7. *Always review and refresh*: Like a solid financial plan, the monitoring and maintenance steps should not be overlooked. New risks will emerge in your life. Adapting to changing circumstances in the here and now can prevent financial disaster years down the road.

Investing is an inherently optimistic act, a belief in a brighter tomorrow. But, paradoxically, we can reduce the risk of our investment decisions by thoughtfully examining possible points of failure before they occur.

Common problems are not holding the appropriate amount of stock market exposure, having insufficient savings or inadequate insurance protection, and not seeking advice from a trusted expert.

It turns out that imagining how bad things can get can be very good indeed.

LISTEN TO
WOMEN

BRITISH CHEMIST AND crystallographer Rosalind Franklin was a young scientist in the 1950s. Her work was partly devoted to producing high-quality X-ray images of DNA fibers. Franklin's most famous image, the iconic Photograph 51, together with her other breakthroughs, provided compelling evidence of DNA's double helix structure.

Franklin's X-ray diffraction experiments and the findings she drew from them were both utilized and then marginalized by her male colleagues. James Watson and Francis Crick—without the permission of Franklin, but relying on her efforts—constructed their own model of DNA's three-dimensional molecular arrangement. Their work was published in 1953, just five years before Franklin's passing from ovarian cancer in 1958 at the age of 37.[195]

It was not until recently that Franklin's work has been recognized for what it was—revolutionary research into the secret of life. The genetics research she conducted would later be grounds for a Nobel Prize award, but Franklin was not among the recipients.[196] It was only posthumously that she began to earn the acclaim she deserved.

It would be easy to write off Franklin's story as being a relic of a bygone sexist era, but data suggest that the same patterns exhibited by Watson and Crick are still true in finance today: We are not listening to women, and we are worse off for it.

While inroads into equality are made each year, it's imperative not to underestimate the valuable contributions of women in male-dominated fields, including financial services and investment management.

The fact is—when it comes to money—women are simply better than men. My former colleague Lara Coviello and I partnered to review the literature on how female investors perform during periods of stock market volatility. It turns out that investing like a woman is a winning strategy. While research shows that women are typically less confident, they outperform men by 1.3 percentage points during bear markets, according to Openfolio.[197] A Wells Fargo study revealed that traits such as discipline, willingness to learn, and careful risk-taking all contribute to their behavioral alpha. While men go with their gut, women tend to take a more measured and research-grounded approach.

The real shocker was unearthed in research by Fidelity. Despite evidence of women's outperformance in both household and professional settings, along with better risk assessment acumen, just 9% of people surveyed, half of whom were women, expect women to beat men in investment management. More concerning is that just 47% of women are confident talking about their money with a professional. New York Life found that 40% of females felt advisors treated them differently, often ignoring what they have to say.[198]

It's stunning that women are often better investors, yet they feel and are seen as subpar compared to men. This is not just a cultural problem. Women are often in a precarious financial position since they tend to live longer than men, while their retirement income is only 83% of men's.[199]

Let's recap: Women generate higher returns than men at the retail level and on Wall Street, they are more disciplined, less impulsive, and generally check their ego at the door while males typically ooze overconfidence. In short, they are the ultimate behavioral investors.

But even to this day, we don't think of women when we picture a sophisticated and experienced fund manager or advisor. According to the CFA Institute, the premiere credentialing institution for asset managers, just 18% of its members are women.[200] Imagine how much better off the financial services industry would be if we just got that number up to 50%.

Beyond the Bloomberg Terminal and stock-picking niche, there's evidence demonstrating that gender diversity on corporate boards leads to improved outcomes.

Research finds that the inclusion of women on boards is associated with higher buyout offers in M&A deals. Women often perform more in-depth analyses and spur thoughtful discussions in the decision-making process.[201] Boards made up of solely men had a whopping 37% higher failure rate than those with directors from both genders, according to a 2021 Australian study.[202]

Like Franklin in the 1950s, women are still overlooked when it comes to major decisions. Despite their financial prowess, they are all too often undermined both in the office and at the kitchen table. Among married couples, 82% of men said they were primarily responsible for making investment changes, while a majority of women, 58%, reported making the more quotidian financial decisions.[203] So, while women have greater parity when it comes to day-to-day financial matters, they dramatically lag men when it comes to executing big investment decisions.

Financial research is often murky with crisscrossing factors at play. But the evidence is unambiguous: Women are fantastic investors, and we would all benefit by them having a seat at the table, no matter what table we are talking about.

YOU DON'T REALLY WANT TO BE RICH, YOU WANT TO BE FREE

REMEMBER THAT OLD series of commercials in which people were toting around large physical numbers? "What's your number?" the narrator would ask, before inviting the viewer to meet with a retirement specialist at the firm to build a financial plan.

Many retirees know full well that retirement isn't about hitting a cold number. In fact, being rich in itself can't bring true joy. Rather, it's having freedom, a sense of significance, personal growth opportunities, and social connections, among other factors, that give us the best shot at contentment.

The Monkey's Paw, a short story written in 1902, illustrates the perils of greed.

In the work, the White family acquires a magical monkey's paw. Its holders are allowed to make three wishes, but each wish would come with diabolical consequences. Mr. White is skeptical of the paw's supposed power and feels like he has his life together. Offhand, he asks for wealth in the sum of £200. The next day, his son Herbert tragically dies in a factory accident, resulting in a £200 cash windfall as compensation.

Mrs. White, grief-stricken, begs her husband to use the talisman to wish their son back to life. Mr. White obliges, though fearful of what may happen, considering his son's body was mutilated in the accident, and the family's second wish is to resurrect their son. Moments pass, and they hear a knock at the front door in the dark of night. Mrs. White rushes to answer, hoping their son beckons, but Mr. White, consumed by fear of what may be standing on their doorstep, impulsively asks that all that has transpired be undone— that's the final wish. Suddenly the knocking stops. Mrs. White opens the door. Nobody is there.

The Whites are left devastated, finding themselves in far worse condition than before they came across the mummified monkey's paw. Instead of delivering monetary blessing, it brought curse. In a broader context, though, it was the White's tampering with fate and desire for just a little bit more abundance that led to their tragic state.

In truth, many of us aspire to reach that next tier of wealth. However, it is all too easy to succumb to the false promise that an extra zero on our salary will cure life's ills. Indeed, 79% of Americans believe more money would bring about a happiness boost.[204] Yet the ability for money to make us happier is complicated, and I discuss it in depth elsewhere in this book. Ultimately, I think that what most people want is not more money per se, but rather the freedom that is thought to accompany it.

When looking through the psychological and philosophical happiness and well-being traditions, freedom and autonomy are everywhere. They are an essential part of almost any research-backed framework for understanding human fulfillment.

Bestselling author and thinker Daniel Pink puts freedom front and center in his MAP framework (Mastery, Autonomy, Purpose) for understanding what drives us. Under this framework, more money means nothing if it comes alongside a loss of independence. While *mastery* involves our desire for personal improvement and *purpose* focuses on discovering meaning in daily life, *autonomy* emphasizes the virtue of self-direction and having the freedom to align your actions with your values.

You might best think of the MAP model in the context of your work life. A truly soul-crushing job would be one in which you have zero knowledge, are micromanaged, and are working for a cause that runs counter to your beliefs.

On the other hand, the perfect vocation feels almost tailored to you—you are the expert in the field (but still have avenues to learn more), have authority over how your time is spent, and build toward some greater purpose.

Freedom is at the heart of your best work life and your best money life.

Besides Pink's framework, other theories and concepts similarly emphasize the fundamental role of freedom.

The Self-Determination Theory (SDT) posits that human motivation and wellness are primarily driven by possessing autonomy, competence, and relatedness. SDT asserts that individuals hold a psychological need for autonomy—having control over one's actions leads to increased life satisfaction.

Existential psychologists, such as Viktor Frankl and Rollo May, argue that just possessing the freedom to choose empowers people to craft their own purpose. Taking away that sense of personal responsibility over an individual's actions in effect robs them of life itself.

The growing field of Positivity Psychology, an area that focuses on understanding human flourishing and well-being, postulates that freedom fosters happiness and life satisfaction—the ability to make choices that align with one's interests is associated with contentment and positive affect.

Frameworks and theories are helpful, but nothing hits the same as feeling first-hand the chasm between richness and freedom. I came across an article featuring one of the ten richest people in the world discussing a standing 9 p.m. work meeting he had with some key lieutenants. I was struck in that moment by just how rich I felt relative to him, even though our bank accounts look vastly different.

Naval Ravikant nicely summed up my feelings when he said, "The ultimate purpose of money is so that you do not have to be in a specific place at a specific time doing anything you don't want to do."

———————

Freedom is a fundamental human desire. It is tightly linked with our happiness, wellness, and flourishing. It's surprising then, that so many of the traditional trappings of wealth do so much to make us unfree. Vacation homes double our upkeep and limit our ability to travel to new places. Fancy cars make us finicky about where to park. Costly timepieces may sit in a case for fear of being scratched or stolen.

I am no ascetic and I like to buy nice things, but examining saving, investing, and spending decisions through the lens of the freedom they afford or demand is a useful rubric for making choices that deliver what will truly make us happy.

NOT CARING WHAT OTHERS THINK IS A VALUABLE ASSET

NIKOLA TESLA WAS a genius who did pioneering work in the development of electric power. He held numerous patents and made significant contributions to breakthroughs in science and technology. But like many savants, the engineer also had an eccentric side, with some downright oddball compulsions that perplexed his peers.

Among his strange habits and rituals was an obsession with pigeons. The Serbian American would spend hours feeding and caring for injured pigeons in New York. Despite being a reported germophobe, he left a window open at his lab to allow pigeons to fly in. He connected with one particular white pigeon, claiming that he fell in love with her.

The peculiarities don't end there. Tesla had a strong aversion to pearls, among other round objects. He refused to speak with women wearing a necklace of pearls and would leave the room at the very sight of such jewelry. Nobody really knows why he hated these gems of the sea.

Third, Tesla displayed compulsive behaviors related to the

number three. He would wash his hands a trio of times and routinely walk three laps around a building before entering. Maybe the most extreme ritual of all was how he handled napkins—Tesla would fold 18 napkins before eating because it was divisible by three.

Unusual sleep habits along with visions and hallucinations were part of his everyday life. He claimed to only require two hours of sleep a night, while some of his inventions were conjured up in his vivid visions and occasional hallucinations.

So deep was Tesla into his research and scientific processes that he never married, fearing that it would interfere with his work, and other personal relationships usually took a back seat to his projects and inventions too. Clearly, some of these peccadilloes were based on obsessive compulsion or something close, but others were a natural extension of a life committed to the field he loved.

Despite, or perhaps because of, his eccentricities, Tesla's contributions to science and engineering were many. He was responsible for developing alternating current (A/C) electrical systems, wireless communication, and other engineering marvels, which continue to influence today's tech-driven world.

Now, I'm not saying that you should fall in love with a pigeon or fold up a bunch of napkins, but I am saying that freeing yourself from the shackles of caring what others think is a powerful way to make better and more personal financial decisions. Tesla was wise in the sense that it is only once we break from trying to impress and conform to the wishes of others that we can truly be free— financially and personally.

One specific area of our finances where we are hampered by our desire to impress others is our overspending.

Just how bad is our tendency to overspend to impress others?

According to a 2022 survey by LendingTree, nearly 40% of

Americans splurge just to show off.[205] The most common spending areas among people in that group were clothing, shoes, accessories, and gifts. Twenty-seven percent of folks busted their budgets enough to bring them into debt, while 77% of respondents expressed regret about going overboard just to impress family, friends, and those Joneses across the street (there they are again!).

The humorist Robert Quillen quipped almost 100 years ago that we are guilty of "using money you haven't earned to buy you things you don't need to impress people you don't like." The things we buy may have changed a bit in the last century, but our behavior certainly has not. And the worst part? It doesn't even work.

Picture yourself on a leisurely Sunday drive. On a warm afternoon with a gentle breeze, you arrive at a red light, and up comes a fancy sports car or a restored classic. You think, "Wow, that's a cool car," as you gaze at its unique design and immaculate sheen, wishing you had the keys to such a beautiful machine. The light turns green, and you both go on your way. Never once did you look at the driver and think, "Wow, that's a cool person!"

This is called the 'spotlight effect', a phenomenon that Morgan Housel observed when working as a valet at a high-end hotel in Los Angeles. Just as in Housel's "man in the car paradox," the cognitive bias asserts that we think people are paying more attention to us than they actually are.[206] The belief causes us to financially overindulge in the hope that others find us 'cool'.[207] In his book, *The Psychology of Money*, Housel sums it up well: "Spending money to show people how much money you have is the fastest way to have less money."

The spotlight effect not only leads to overspending, but social anxiety and poorer overall mental health are also common results. The bias is driven by egocentric tendencies and the 'anchoring effect', whereby we rely too heavily on our own perspectives and initial information. Individuals then tend to overestimate how much others notice variations in their behavior or appearance.

Being aware of this bias can help us make more balanced judgments and avoid unnecessary anxiety, but like so many behavioral quirks, simply being aware of them does not make you immune to them.

To recap, the urge to overspend on clothes and cars is often fueled by a misguided belief that people are closely scrutinizing us. In reality, they are thinking of themselves, just like you are. Meanwhile, spending to make our ego happy is an action we almost always regret.

———————

How can we break free from this cycle?
Try these on for size:

- **Focus on personal growth and acceptance**: Needing to impress others is emblematic of a conditional sense of self. As you begin to realize that you are enough, the need to impress begins to fall away.
- **Limit exposure to social media**: These platforms are a conformity factory, producing a culture of comparison, leading to individual feelings of inadequacy. Reducing your time on social media can help improve your overall well-being and decrease the desire to impress based on unrealistic standards. Research has found that people who throttled back their social media usage to just ten minutes per platform daily showed significant drops in depression and loneliness.[208] Those two conditions commonly result in retail therapy in a fruitless effort to boost social standing in our minds.
- **Experiment with creativity**: While impressing others is almost necessarily an act in conformity, creativity is the opposite; the building of something new and heretofore non-existent. As you begin to create your reality instead of parroting others', your perspective will shift.

- **Find your community:** The company you keep greatly influences your behavior, so choose friends who truly appreciate and accept you for who you are, without the need for constant impressing. Jack Kerouac described such friends as "the mad ones, the ones who are mad to live, mad to talk, mad to be saved, desirous of everything at the same time, the ones that never yawn or say a commonplace thing, but burn, burn, burn like fabulous yellow roman candles." With friends like that, you'll experience an exhilarating journey of self-discovery and fulfillment.

A desire to belong is among the most primal and natural human yearnings. It's not good to be alone but belonging to a group based on superficialities will never satisfy you. By finding people with whom we connect around big ideas, creativity, and shared values, we can avoid the vapid solipsism of needing to spend to be accepted.

NO ONE GETS
RICH ALONE

AMONG THE MOST cherished American virtues is the willingness of individuals to pull themselves up by their bootstraps and earn financial success through hard work. Who doesn't love a self-made millionaire story filled with challenges overcome and ambitions fulfilled? It's no coincidence that these inspiring narratives are everywhere in popular television and movies.

Being emboldened to go your own way is at the heart of the American spirit. It offends us as red-blooded Americans when we get told that what we've worked so hard for isn't at the sole doing of our elbow grease. Never was this seen more clearly than in the 2012 presidential campaign. Those infamous words by then-candidate Barack Obama, "If you've got a business, you didn't build that," caused an immediate firestorm. The line went viral even during those early years of social media.

The political right chastised Obama for such a dismissive tone against hardworking entrepreneurs, while the left said the line was more about the benefits of domestic infrastructure rather than a negation of personal excellence.

Whatever side of the political aisle you're on, it's undeniable that true wealth is often built collectively. Behavioral science suggests that we tend to underestimate environmental factors and overestimate our own talent when we form a mental mosaic of how we got to where we are today.

What does the greatest investor of all time have to say about the issue? Warren Buffett once described how he won the "ovarian lottery" by being born in the United States, where his capitalistic intuition and analytical prowess are rewarded best. He'd likely be a nobody had he been born in the developing world. And what might his career have been like had he been born in 1830 or 2020 instead of 1930? His early adult years were at the very ideal times to be an American capitalist in a soon-to-thrive stock market era.

Let's not forget about all you bond lovers out there. Bill Gross, the "Bond King," launched his career right near the time of max interest rates. Starting out in finance during the volatile 1970s, the bulk of his asset management tenure coincided with a fixed income boom. The 10-year Treasury rate steadily declined from near 16% in the early 1980s to under 2% by 2012. That four-decade bull market in bonds was undoubtedly a tailwind for Gross.

None of this is meant to throw shade on the brilliance of Buffett and Gross. It simply underscores that the right place and time play important roles in how our financial lives are shaped. If you are wealthy, you must be extra diligent about checking your ego at the door.

Studies show that relatively wealthy people tend to overattribute their wealth to their own perceived greatness while minimizing external factors. Adding a dose of humility along our money journey can improve our mindset.

According to research out of the University of California at Berkeley, luxury car owners are more likely to perform selfish—even dangerous—acts on the road. When studying how likely someone in a car was to yield to a pedestrian, those in fancier cars were less likely to stop for those approaching the crosswalk. Watch out for those Bimmers and Benzes the next time you need to cross the street! The paper goes beyond hot wheels and finds that wealthy individuals are often less empathetic, which is another factor that causes them to overlook the contributions of others toward their success.

We can all look back and spot key moments in our lives that reshaped our financial situation. A big promotion at work, an encounter with what would turn out to be an influential mentor, or a helping hand from a family member when you were down on your luck. But it is the not-so-obvious conditions that we tend to discount when tallying our financial success.

Socioeconomic factors, such as race, gender, and even class still play crucial roles in how our financial lives unfold. The advantages of quality education, access to healthcare, and being around smart and motivated people early in life can separate the haves from the have-nots—and those are often uncontrollable variables for far too many people.

Simply acknowledging the role of luck and chance is a key step toward humbling yourself. Having empathy and compassion for those less fortunate who have not been blessed with the same opportunities brings everyone together and helps to reduce systemic inequalities that threaten the long-term financial health of the economy writ large. Practicing gratitude and giving back benefits you and future generations so that more people have the chance to reach their financial goals.

Success with money is always a combination of both luck and effort. It is crucial to remember that interplay and recognize the contributions of others, as well as bigger uncontrollable factors, as we progress in life and to keep a keen eye out for opportunities to lend a helping hand once we have achieved success.

French songstress and actress Edith Piaf said it best, "When you reach the top, you should remember to send the elevator back down for the others."

ENDNOTES

1   Lydia Saad, "Seven in 10 Americans Likely to Set Goals for 2023," GALLUP (January 5, 2023).

2   Beverlee Warren, "The Top Five Regrets of the Dying: A Life Transformed by the Dearly Departing by Bronnie Ware," *Baylor University Medical Center Proceedings* (2012).

3   "PERMA™ Theory Of Well-Being And PERMA™ Workshops," Positive Psychology Center, University of Pennsylvania, School of Arts and Sciences.

4   Elizabeth W. Dunn, Lara B. Aknin, and Michael I. Norton, "Spending money on others promotes happiness," *Science* (2008).

5   Soyoung Q. Park, Thorsten Kahnt, Azade Dogan, Sabrina Strang, Ernst Fehr, and Philippe N. Tobler, "A neural link between generosity and happiness," Vol. 8 *Nature Communications* (2017).

6   John F. Helliwell, Haifang Huang, Shun Wang Professor, and Max Norton, "Happiness, Benevolence, and Trust During COVID-19 and Beyond," World Happiness Report (March 18, 2022).

7   L. B. Aknin, C. P. Barrington-Leigh, E. W. Dunn, J. F. Helliwell, J. Burns, R. Biswas-Diene, I. Kemeza, P. Nyende, C. E. Ashton-James, and M. I. Norton, "Prosocial spending and well-being: Cross-cultural evidence for a psychological universal," *Journal of Personality and Social Psychology*, Vol. 104:4 (2013), 635–652.

8   Lara B. Aknin, J. Kiley Hamlin, and Elizabeth W. Dunn, "Giving Leads to Happiness in Young Children," *PLoS ONE*, Vol. 7:6 (June 14, 2012).

9   Ken Honda, *Happy Money: The Japanese Art of Making Peace with Your Money* (Simon & Schuster, 2014).

10   Emily Sohn, "Why the Great Molasses Flood Was So Deadly," history.com (January 15, 2019).

11 "Doing makes you happier than owning – even before buying," *Cornell Chronicle*, Cornell University (September 2, 2014).

12 Anthony P. Carnevale, Stephen J. Rose and Ban Cheah, "The College Payoff," The Georgetown University Center on Education and the Workforce (2011).

13 Ann Garcia, *How To Pay For College* (Harriman House, 2022).

14 Amanda Bucceri Androus, "Here's How Much Your Healthcare Costs Will Rise as You Age," RegisteredNursing.org (September 8, 2023).

15 "How to plan for rising health care costs," Fidelity (June 21, 2023).

16 Tim Brinkhof, "The real reason Vincent van Gogh cut off his ear," BigThink (April 21, 2023).

17 W. M. Runyan, "Why did Van Gogh cut off his ear? The problem of alternative explanations in psychobiography," *Journal of Personality and Social Psychology* (June 1981).

18 Matt Suwak, "Conquer Self-Doubt With Vincent van Gogh," FactoryTwoFour (May 20, 2021).

19 Dietrich Blumer, "The Illness of Vincent van Gogh," *The American Journal of Psychiatry*, Vol. 159:4 (April 1, 2002).

20 Maev Kennedy, "Van Gogh 'cut off his ear after learning brother was to marry'," *Guardian* (October 31, 2016).

21 Lingxi Gao, Bochi Sun, Ziqing Du, and Guangming Lv, "How Wealth Inequality Affects Happiness: The Perspective of Social Comparison," *Frontiers in Psychology*, Vol. 13 (April 11, 2022).

22 "Social comparisons drive income's effect on happiness in states with higher inequality," *ScienceDaily*, University of Illinois at Urbana-Champaign (April 13, 2021).

23 Matt Johnson, "How Social Comparison Drives Our Happiness, Wealth, and Social Media Status," neuroscienceof.com.

24 Joshua Brown and Joel Wong, "How Gratitude Changes You and Your Brain," *Greater Good Magazine*, Berkeley, University of California (June 6, 2017).

25 Mingli Liu, Kimberly E. Kamper-DeMarco, Jie Zhang, Jia Xiao, Daifeng Dong, and Peng Xue, "Time Spent on Social Media and Risk of Depression in Adolescents: A Dose–Response Meta-Analysis," *International Journal of Environmental Research and Public Health*, Vol.19:9 (April 24, 2022).

26 www.imdb.com

27 www.usps.com

28 www.firmsofendearment.com

29 Victor J. Strecher, "Finding Purpose and Meaning In Life: Living for What Matters Most," University of Michigan.

30 Victor J. Strecher, *Life on Purpose: How Living for What Matters Most Changes Everything* (HarpeOne, 2016).

31 Caleb Naysmith, "Blockbuster Had The Opportunity To Buy Netflix For $50 Million But 'Laughed Them Out Of The Room': A $150 Billion Mistake," Benzinga (May 25, 2023).

32 John Corrigan, "How many unused vacation days do Americans leave on the table?" *Human Resouces Director* (December 12, 2022).

33 Joyce Marter, "How to Prevent Overwork and Burnout," *Psychology Today* (July 11, 2021).

34 Davide Di Gioia, Anu R. Ganti, Craig Lazzara, and Grace Stoddart, "SPIVA U.S. Mid-Year 2023," S&P Dow Jones Indices (September 21, 2023).

35 Benjamin Graham and Jason Zweig, *The Intelligent Investor* (Harper Business, 2006).

36 Robin Liefeld, "Clothing Optional: Victor Hugo's Unconventional Writing," Medium.com (September 20, 2023).

37 Benjamin Gardner, Phillippa Lally, and Jane Wardle, "Making health habitual: the psychology of 'habit-formation' and general practice," *British Journal of General Practice*, Vol. 62:605 (December 2012).

38 Peter J. Bayley, Jennifer C. Frascino, and Larry R. Squire, "Robust habit learning in the absence of awareness and independent of the medial temporal lobe," *Nature*, Vol. 436:7050 (July 28, 2005).

39 C. L. Hull, "Principles of behavior: An introduction to behavior theory," American Psychological Association (1943).

40 Phillippa Lally, Cornelia H. M. van Jaarsveld, Henry W. W. Potts, and Jane Wardle, "How are habits formed: Modelling habit formation in the real world," *European Journal of Social Psychology*, Vol. 40:6 (July 16, 2009).

41 Benjamin Gardner, Phillippa Lally, and Jane Wardle, "Making health habitual: The psychology of 'habit-formation' and general practice," *British Journal of General Practice*, Vol. 62:605 (December 2012).

42 Ibid.

43 Ferris Jabr, "Does Thinking Really Hard Burn More Calories?" *Scientific American* (July 18, 2012).

44 Erin Lowell, "How Much Should I Budget for Eating Out?" YNAB (January 26, 2022).

45 "World Obesity Atlas 2023," World Obesity Federation (March 2023).

46 "Tobacco," WHO (July 31, 2023).

47 "Doctors, Nurses and Smoking: Understanding Smoking Among Medical Professionals," Tobaccofreelife.org.

48 Ilana Boivie and Nari Rhee, "The Continuing Retirement Savings Crisis," National Institute on Retirement Security (March 2015).

49 Rohit Chopra, "As outstanding credit card debt hits new high, the CFPB is focusing on ways to increase competition and reduce costs," Consumer financial Protection Bureau (April 17, 2023).

50 Jessica Dickler, "With 62% of Americans living paycheck to paycheck amid inflation, more people have a side job," CNBC (March 28, 2023).

51 Jeffrey Pfeffer and Robert I. Sutton, *The Knowing-Doing Gap: How Smart Companies Turn Knowledge into Action* (Harvard Business School Press, 2000).

52 Samantha Lamas and Ray Sin, "Behavioral Nudges for Goals-Based Financial Planning," Morningstar.

53 Dilip Soman and Amar Cheema, "Earmarking and Partitioning: Increasing Saving by Low-Income Households," *Journal of Marketing Research*, Vol. XLVIII (November 2011), S14–S22.

54 "Goals-based investing in volatile markets," SEI (September 28, 2022).

55 J. Bomyea, H. Ramsawh, T. M. Ball, C. T. Taylor, M. P. Paulus, A. J. Lang, and M. B. Stein, "Intolerance of uncertainty as a mediator of reductions in worry in a cognitive behavioral treatment program for generalized anxiety disorder," *Journal of Anxiety Disorders*, Vol. 33 (June 2015).

56 Nicholas Carleton, "Fear of the unknown: One fear to rule them all? Author links open overlay panel," *Journal of Anxiety Disorders*, Vol. 41 (June 2016), 5–21.

57 Christian C. Luhmann, Kanako Ishida, and Greg Hajcak, "Intolerance of Uncertainty and Decisions About Delayed, Probabilistic Rewards," *Behavior Therapy*, Vol. 42:3 (September 2011), 378–386.

58 Mike Zaccardi, "Chart of the Week: Quarantined Cash," topdowncharts.com (May 12, 2020).

59 Ben Carlson, "The Long-Term Wins," Awealthofcommonsense.com (January 15, 2023).

60 Bob Pisani, "Long-term investors shouldn't worry too much about stocks being 10% off their highs," CNBC (January 25, 2022).

61 "The Greatest American Novels you should read," penguin.co.uk (November 19, 2020).

62 Daniel Kahneman and Angus Deaton, "High Income Improves Evaluation of Life But Not Emotional Well-Being," *Proceedings of the National Academy of Sciences*, Vol. 107:38 (September 2010), 16489– 16493.

63 Michele W. Berger, "Does Money Buy Happiness? Here's What the Research Says," *Knowledge at Wharton*, Wharton, University of Pennsylvania (March 28, 2023).

64 Sonja Lyubomirsky, Kennon M. Sheldon, and David Schkade, "Pursuing Happiness: The Architecture of Sustainable Change," *Review of General Psychology*, Vol. 9:2 (2005), 111–131.

65 Kira M. Newman, "How Much of Your Happiness is Under Your Control?" *Greater Good Magazine*, University of California, Berkeley (February 18, 2020).

66 Laura Silver, Patrick van Kessel, Christine Huang, Laura Clancy, and Sneha Gubbala, "What Makes Life Meaningful? Views From 17 Advanced Economies," Pew Research Center (November 18, 2021).

67 Anna Miller, "Can this marriage be saved?" *Monitor on Psychology*, 44:4, American Psychological Association (April 2013).

68 Isabel V. Sawhill, Morgan Welch, and Chris Miller, "It's getting more expensive to raise children: And government isn't doing much to help," The Brookings Institution (August 30, 2022).

69 Alan D. Blotcky, "The toll of parental alienation on children," *Contemporary Pediatrics* (April 8, 2022).

70 Matthew Zane, "What Percentage of People Are Fired?" Zippia (March 3, 2023).

71 ECMC Group.

72 "Survival of private sector establishments by opening year," bls.gov.

73 Lyle Daly, "U.S. Millionaires and Billionaires: You Might Not Believe the Wealth," *The Motley Fool* (March 15, 2023).

74 "60% of Americans Now Living Paycheck to Paycheck, Down from 64% a Month Ago," LendingClub (February 28, 2023).

75 Andrea Koczela, "Ten Facts You Should Know about Albert Einstein," BooksTellYouWhy.com (March 12, 2014).

76 "Einstein: Renowned Genius, Tabloid Dream," ABC News (April 10, 2007).

77 "Financial Self-Improvement: Exploring Americans' Perception of Their Financial Strengths and Weaknesses," couponfollow.com.

78 Ryan Ermey, "98% of Americans have at least 1 money bias, research finds — and it's costing them," CNBC (January 14, 2022).

79 "Stress in America," American Psychological Association.

80 Benjamin E. Hilbig, "Good Things Don't Come Easy (to Mind)," *Experimental Psychology* (July 2012).

81 "Want to exercise more? You're much more likely to stick with an activity you enjoy," The Muscle Clinic (January 15, 2017).

82   Jo Salmon, Neville Owen, David Crawford, Adrian Bauman, and James F Sallis, "Physical activity and sedentary behavior: A population-based study of barriers, enjoyment, and preference," *Health Psychology*, Vol. 22:2 (March 2003).

83   David Noonan, "Failure Found to Be an 'Essential Prerequisite' for Success," *Scientific American* (October 30, 2019).

84   Jeremy Adam Smith, "How to Learn From Your Failures," *Greater Good Magazine*, University of California, Berkeley (August 24, 2022).

85   Nachum Sicherman, George Loewenstein, Duane J. Seppi, and Stephen P. Utkus, "Financial Attention," Oxford University Press on behalf of The Society for Financial Studies (2015).

86   Ben Carlson, "How Often Should You Expect a Stock Market Correction?" *A Wealth of Common Sense* (January 20, 2022).

87   Brad M. Barber, Yong-Ill Lee, Yu-Jane Liu Peking, and Terrance Odean, "Do Day Traders Rationally Learn About Their Ability?" (January 2014).

88   Nicholas A. Christakis and James H. Fowler, "The Spread of Obesity in a Large Social Network over 32 Years," *The New England Journal of Medicine*, Vol. 357 (2007), 370-379.

89   Jean Baldwin Grossman and Joseph P. Tierney, "Does mentoring work? An impact study of the Big Brothers Big Sisters program," *Evaluation Review*, Vol. 22:3 (1998), 403–426.

90   Thomas Niederkrotenthaler, Arno Herberth, and Gernot Sonneck, "The 'Werther-effect': Legend or Reality?" *Neuropsychiatry*, Vol. 21:4 (2007), 284–290.

91   Nicholas A. Christakis and James H. Fowler, "The Collective Dynamics of Smoking in a Large Social Network List of Authors," *The New England Journal of Medicine*, Vol. 358 (2008), 2249–2258.

92   David Burkus, "You're NOT The Average Of The Five People You Surround Yourself With," Medium.com (May 23, 2018).

93   Cheryl D. Fryar, Jeffery P. Hughes, Kirsten A. Herrick, and Namanjeet Ahluwalia, "Fast Food Consumption Among Adults in the United States, 2013–2016," NCHS Data Brief No. 322 (October 2018).

94   Lauren Hirsch, Ephrat Livni, Sarah Kessler, and Bernhard Warner, "Why Do Almost Half of Americans Leave Paid Time Off on the Table?" *The New York Times* (May 27, 2023).

95   John Corrigan, "How many unused vacation days do Americans leave on the table?" *Human Resources Director* (December 12, 2022).

96   David Dunning, "Self-Insight: Roadblocks and Detours on the Path to Knowing Thyself," *Psychology Press* (2005).

97 "Four Simple Ways to Apply EAST Framework to Behavioural Insights," The Behavioral Insights Team.

98 https://www.chicagobooth.edu/review/save-more-tomorrow.

99 Lenka H. Shriver, Barbara J. Marriage, Tama D. Bloch, Colleen K. Spees, Samantha A. Ramsay, Rosanna P. Watowicz, and Christopher A. Taylor, "Contribution of snacks to dietary intakes of young children in the United States," *Maternal & Child Nutrition*, Vol. 14:1 (2018).

100 Giovanni Sogari, Catalina Velez-Argumedo, Miguel I. Gómez, and Cristina Mora, "College Students and Eating Habits: A Study Using an Ecological Model for Healthy Behavior," *Nutrients*, Vol. 10:12 (December).

101 "New Research Finds Link Between Financial Status and Body Weight," Association for Financial Counseling & Planning Education.

102 "Benefits of Physical Activity," Centers for Disease Control and Prevention.

103 "How to save money and feel happier," *The Globe and Mail* (October 7, 2019).

104 Sonya Britt, "The Intergenerational Transfer of Money Attitudes and Behaviors," *Journal of Consumer Affairs* (2016).

105 Jinhee Kim, Jaslean LaTaillade, and Haejeong Kim, "Family processes and adolescents' financial behaviors," *Journal of Family and Economic Issues*, Vol. 32:4 (2011), 668–679.

106 Jinhee Kim and Swarn Chatterjee, "Childhood financial socialization and young adults' financial management," *Journal of Financial Counseling and Planning*, Vol. 24:1 (2013), 61–79.

107 Adam Hancock, Bryce Jorgensen, and Melvin Swanson, "College Students and Credit Card Use: The Role of Parents, Work Experience, Financial Knowledge, and Credit Card Attitudes," *Journal of Family and Economic Issues*, Springer, Vol. 34:4 (2013), 369–381.

108 Soyeon Shim 1, Bonnie L Barber, Noel A Card, Jing Jian Xiao, and Joyce Serido, "Financial socialization of first-year college students: The roles of parents, work, and education," *Journal of Youth and Adolescence*, Vol. 39:12 (2010).

109 Bradley Klontz, Sonya L. Britt, and Kristy L. Archuleta, "Disordered Money Behaviors: Development of the Klontz Money Behavior Inventory," *Journal of Financial Therapy*, Vol. 3:1 (2012).

110 Robert A. Emmons and Michael E. McCullough, "Counting Blessings Versus Burdens: An Experimental Investigation of Gratitude and Subjective Well-Being in Daily Life," *Journal of Personality and Social Psychology*, Vol. 84:2 (2003), 377–389.

111 Fred B. Bryant and Joseph Veroff, "Savoring: A new model of positive experience," American Psychological Association (2007).

112 Kira M. Newman, "Is Social Connection the Best Path to Happiness?" *Greater Good Magazine*, University of California, Berkeley (June 27, 2018).

113 Benjamin Graham and Jason Zweig, *The Intelligent Investor* (Harper Business, 2006), p. 374.

114 Christopher H. Browne, *The Little Book of Value Investing* (Wiley, 2006).

115 Burton Malkiel, *A Random Walk Down Wall Street* (W. W. Norton & Company, 2020).

116 Jeff Sommer, "Clueless About 2020, Wall Street Forecasters Are at It Again for 2021," *The New York Times* (December 18, 2020).

117 Tim Kasser and Kennon M. Sheldon, "Time Affluence as a Path toward Personal Happiness and Ethical Business Practice: Empirical Evidence from Four Studies," *Journal of Business Ethics*, Vol. 84 (2009), 243–255.

118 Ashley V. Whillans, Aaron C. Weidman, and Elizabeth W. Dunn, "Valuing time over money is associated with greater happiness," *Social Psychological and Personality Science*, Vol. 7:3 (2016), 213–222.

119 Ashley V. Whillans, Elizabeth W. Dunn, Paul Smeets, and Michael I. Norton, "Buying time promotes happiness," *Proceedings of the National Academy of Sciences*, Vol. 114:32 (July 24, 2017).

120 Tanza Loudenback, "Study: Adding 20 Minutes to Your Commute Makes You as Miserable as Getting a 19 Percent Pay Cut," Inc.com (October 23, 2017).

121 Brett McKay and Kate McKay, "What the Race to the South Pole Can Teach You About How to Achieve Your Goals," The Art of Manliness (April 22, 2012).

122 Denise T. D. de Ridder, Gerty Lensvelt-Mulders, Catrin Finkenauer, F. Marijn Stok, and Roy F. Baumeister, "Taking stock of self-control: A meta-analysis of how trait self-control relates to a wide range of behaviors," *Personality and Social Psychology Review*, Vol. 16:1 (2012), 76–99.

123 Wilhelm Hofmann, Roy F. Baumeister, Georg Förster, and Kathleen D. Vohs, "Everyday temptations: an experience sampling study of desire, conflict, and self-control," *Journal of Personality and Social Psychology*, Vol. 102:6 (2012), 1318–1335.

124 Marina Milyavskaya and Michael Inzlicht, "What's So Great About Self-Control? Examining the Importance of Effortful Self-Control and Temptation in Predicting Real-Life Depletion and Goal Attainment," *Social Psychological and Personality Science*, Vol. 8:6 (2017).

125 Angela L. Duckworth, Katherine L. Milkman, and David Laibson, "Beyond Willpower: Strategies for Reducing Failures of Self-Control," *Psychological Science in the Public Interest*, Vol. 19:3 (February 13, 2019).

126 Veronika Job, Gregory M. Walton, Katharina Bernecker, and Carol S. Dweck, "Implicit theories about willpower predict self-regulation and grades in everyday life," *Journal of Personality and Social Psychology*, Vol. 108:4 (2015), 637–647.

127 N. N. Taleb, *Antifragile* (Random House, 2014).

128 "Investment Company Fact Book," Investment Company Institute (2023).

129 Joe Pappalardo, "New Transatlantic Cable Built to Shave 5 Milliseconds off Stock Trades," *Popular Mechanics* (October 27, 2011).

130 "Stress in America 2022," American Psychological Association.

131 "New Payoff Study Finds Nearly 1 in 4 Americans and 1 in 3 Millennials Suffer From PTSD-Like Symptoms Caused by Financially Induced Stress," *Business Wire* (April 20, 2016).

132 Russell W. Belk, "Three Scales to Measure Constructs Related to Materialism: Reliability, Validity, and Relationships to Measures of Happiness," *Advances in Consumer Research*, Vol. 11 (1984), 291–297.

133 Helga Dittmar, Rod Bond, Megan Hurst, and Tim Kasser, "The relationship between materialism and personal well-being: A meta-analysis," *Journal of Personality and Social Psychology*, Vol. 107:5 (2014), 879–924.

134 Emma L. Bradshaw, James H. Conigrave, Ben A. Steward, Kelly A. Ferber, Philip D. Parker, and Richard M. Ryan, "A meta-analysis of the dark side of the American dream: Evidence for the universal wellness costs of prioritizing extrinsic over intrinsic goals," *Journal of Personality and Social Psychology*, Vol. 124:4 (2023), 873–899.

135 Tim Kasser and Richard M. Ryan, "A dark side of the American dream: Correlates of financial success as a central life aspiration," *Journal of Personality and Social Psychology*, Vol. 65:2 (1993), 410–422.

136 Lisa Ryan and Suzanne Dziurawiec, "Materialism and Its Relationship to Life Satisfaction," *Social Indicators Research*, Vol. 55:2 (2001), 185–197.

137 M. Joseph Sirgy, "Materialism and Quality of Life," *Social Indicators Research*, Vol. 43 (1998), 227–260.

138 Martin E. P. Seligman, Tracy A Steen, Nansook Park, and Christopher Peterson, "Positive Psychology Progress: Empirical Validation of Interventions," *American Psychologist*, Vol. 60:5 (July 2005), 410–421.

139 "Giving thanks can make you happier," Harvard (August 14, 2021).

140 Courtney E. Ackerman, "Benefits of Gratitude: 28+ Surprising Research Findings," positivepsychology.com (April 12, 2017).

141 "Giving thanks can make you happier," Harvard (August 14, 2021).

142 S.-T. Cheng, P. K. Tsui, and J. H. M. Lam, "Improving Mental Health in Health Care Practitioners: Randomized Controlled Trial of a Gratitude Intervention," *Journal of Consulting and Clinical Psychology*, Vol. 83 (2015), 177–186.

143 Bryan J. Dik, Ryan D. Duffy, Blake A. Allan, Maeve B. O'Donnell, Yerin Shim, and Michael F. Steger, "Purpose and meaning in career development applications," *The Counseling Psychologist*, Vol. 43:4 (2015), 558–585.

144 David DeSteno, Ye Li, Leah Dickens, and Jennifer S. Lerner, "Gratitude: A Tool for Reducing Economic Impatience," *Psychological Science*, Vol. 25:6 (April 23, 2014).

145 Robert Exley Jr., "Set goals and automated withdrawals to boost your savings by more than 70%, a financial psychologist says," CNBC (December 29, 2021).

146 Saloni Dattani, Lucas Rodés-Guirao, Hannah Ritchie, Esteban Ortiz-Ospina, and Max Roser, "Life Expectancy," ourworldindata.org.

147 "Global Health Then and Now," World101 (February 24, 2023).

148 Aaron O'Neill, "Child mortality rate (under five years old) in the United States, from 1800 to 2020," Statista (June 21, 2022).

149 David Rosnick, "A History of Poverty Worldwide," Center for Economic and Policy Research (May 21, 2019).

150 "Motor vehicle fatality rate in U.S. by year," Wikipedia.

151 "Annual working hours per worker," ourworldindata.org.

152 Cam, "The Feynman Technique," A&S Academic Advising and Coaching, University of Colorado, Boulder (August 7, 2020).

153 Deborah A. Cobb-Clark, Sonja C. Kassenboehmer, Mathias G. Sinning, "Locus of control and savings," *Journal of Banking & Finance*, Vol. 73 (December 2016), 113–130.

154 Tim Fallaw, "What's Your Role In Your Financial Outcomes?" DataPoints (September 13, 2022).

155 The Human Side of Money podcast, Ep. 30, "Exploring The Mindsets and Motivations Driving Money Decisions with Rachel Cruze."

156 Maurie Backman, "You don't need that: Average American spends almost $18,000 a year on nonessentials," *USA Today*.

157 Susan Stamberg, "How Andrew Carnegie Turned His Fortune Into A Library Legacy," NPR (August 1, 2013).

158 "Andrew Carnegie," Carnegie Mellon University.

159 Sandra C. Matz, Joe J. Gladstone, and David Stillwell, "Money Buys Happiness When Spending Fits Our Personality," *Psychological Science*, Vol. 27:5 (2016).

160   Marie-Claire Eylott, "Mary Anning: the unsung hero of fossil discovery," Natural History Museum.

161   SPIVA, S&P Global.

162   Diarmuid Coughlan, Pedro F. Saint-Maurice, Susan A. Carlson, Janet Fulton, and Charles E. Matthews, "Leisure time physical activity throughout adulthood is associated with lower medicare costs: evidence from the linked NIH-AARP diet and health study cohort," *BMJ Open Sport & Exercise Medicine*, Vol. 7:1 (2021).

163   Guido Cozzi, Silvia Galli, and Noemi Mantovan, "Will a shrink make you richer? Gender differences in the effects of psychotherapy on labour efficiency," *European Economic Review*, Vol. 109 (October 2018), 257–274.

164   Anton James Duvall, "Calculating a mentor's effect on salary and retention," *Financial Management* (December 1, 2016).

165   Stephanie Mansfield, "Inside the World's Richest Rivalry: Doris Duke and Barbara Hutton," *Town & Country* (April 26, 2017).

166   Patrick F. Fagan, Kirk A. Johnson, and Jonathan Butcher, "The Map of the Family," The Heritage Foundation.

167   Julia A. Heath and B. F. Kiker, "Determinants of Spells of Poverty Following Divorce," *Review of Social Economy*, Vol. 50:3 (1992), 305–315.

168   "Effects of Divorce on Financial Stability," Marripedia.

169   "Divorce and Money Study," Fidelity.

170   Bespoke Investment Group, "Strategists' 2008 S&P 500 Price Targets," Seeking Alpha (July 23, 2008).

171   "Putting a value on your value: Quantifying Advisor's Alpha," Vanguard (August 12, 2022).

172   "2019 Value of an Adviser Report," Russell Investments.

173   "How Hyundai Sells More When Everyone Else Is Selling Less," Knowledge at Wharton (June 10, 2009).

174   Kristina Monllos, "'Right thing to do at the right time': The definitive oral history of Hyundai's assurance program," Digiday (March 31, 2020).

175   Dale Buss, "Hyundai Reprises 'Assurance' Program For Coronavirus Era," *Forbes* (March 31, 2020).

176   Maurie Backman, "Does the Average American Have a 401(k)?" *The Motley Fool* (June 19, 2017).

177   Megan Leonhardt, "Only a third of Americans say they avoid this investment mistake," CNBC (May 17, 2019)

178   Michael Jones, "Life Insurance Statistics and Industry Trends To Know in 2023," Annuity.org (October 16, 2023).

179 Rob Williams, "5 Ways Financial Planning Can Help," Charles Schwab (January 13, 2022).

180 Piotr Bialowolski, Dorota Weziak-Bialowolska, Matthew T. Lee, Ying Chen, Tyler J. VanderWeele, and Eileen McNeely, "The role of financial conditions for physical and mental health. Evidence from a longitudinal survey and insurance claims data," *Social Science & Medicine*, Vol. 281 (July 2021).

181 "Big-Picture Thinking Leads to the Right Money Mindset," Capital One (January 27, 2020).

182 Meghan C. Evans, Mohsen Bazargan, Sharon Cobb, and Shervin Assari, "Mental and Physical Health Correlates of Financial Difficulties Among African-American Older Adults in Low-Income Areas of Los Angeles," *Front Public Health*, Vol. 8:21 (2020).

183 "Financial stress is hurting relationships, well-being & organizational success," BrightPlan, 2023 Wellness Barometers Survey.

184 Willis Towers Watson.

185 "Exercise and Salary: Exercising Regularly Leads to Receiving Better Pay," Real Men Real Style (December 4, 2023).

186 Maddie Shepherd, "Local Shopping Statistics: Facts on Buying Local," Fundera by NerdWallet (January 23, 2023).

187 Aswath Damodaran, "Historical Returns on Stocks, Bonds and Bills: 1928–2023," NYU Stern.

188 Steven H. Chapman, Mitchell P. LaPlante, and Gail Wilensky, "Life Expectancy and Health Status of the Aged," *Social Security Bulletin*, Vol. 49:10 (October 1986).

189 Tristan McConnell, "Today's 5-year-olds will likely live to 100. What will their lives be like?" *National Geographic* (February 24, 2023).

190 Rob Williams, "5 Ways Financial Planning Can Help," Charles Schwab (January 13, 2022).

191 Herb Weisbaum, "Here's what happens when you miss your credit card payments," NBC (August 28, 2018).

192 Risa Gelles-Watnick and Andrew Perrin, "Who doesn't read books in America?" Pew Research Center (September 21, 2021).

193 Quoctrung Bui and Claire Cain Miller, "The Typical American Lives Only 18 Miles From Mom," *The New York Times* (December 23, 2015).

194 "Where are meme stock investors now? Ally survey finds the majority still own a meme stock," ally.com (February 18, 2022).

195 Matthew Cobb and Nathaniel Comfort, "What Rosalind Franklin truly contributed to the discovery of DNA's structure," *Nature* (April 25, 2023).

196 Reed Jones, "Sexism in Science: Was Rosalind Franklin Robbed of a Nobel Prize?" *LMU This Week*, Loyola Marymount University (March 22, 2021).

197 Dr. Daniel Crosby and Lara Coviello, "Why Women Are The Ultimate Behavioral Investors," *FA* (August 24, 2022).

198 R. J. Shook, "Women Feel Ignored By Advisors, Study Says," *Forbes* (August 7, 2020).

199 Lyle Daly, "Investing for Women: What You Should Know," *The Motley Fool* (September 26, 2023).

200 "Women In Investment Management Initiative," CFA Institute.

201 Stevo Pavićević , Jerayr (John) Haleblian, and Thomas Keil, "When Do Boards of Directors Contribute to Shareholder Value in Firms Targeted for Acquisition? A Group Information-Processing Perspective," *Organization Science*, Vol. 34:5 (November 14, 2022).

202 Matt Wade and Monica Attia, "View from the top: Why having women in the boardroom gives companies a boost," *The Sydney Morning Herald* (February 6, 2022).

203 "How men and women really divide financial responsibilities," InvestmentNews.

204 Joshua Becker, "79% Of Americans Believe More Money Will Make Them Happier: Here's Why They're Wrong," *Forbes* (April 26, 2022).

205 Jacqueline DeMarco, Dan Shepard, and Pearly Huang, "Keeping Up With the Joneses: Nearly 40% of Americans Overspend to Impress Others; Most Want to 'Feel Successful'," Lending Tree (August 29, 2022).

206 "Personal Finance Advice: Beware of 'The Man in Car' Paradox," YouTube.

207 "Why do we feel like we stand out more than we really do?" The Decision Lab.

208 Michele W. Berger, "Social media use increases depression and loneliness," *Penn Today* (November 9, 2018).

ACKNOWLEDGMENTS

Writing a book is a time-consuming, maddening affair that causes you to ignore some of the most important people in your life. Here are the people I ignored to write this book, who are still around:

- Katrina – for the beautiful lens on life and keeping it all together
- Charlotte – for your example, music suggestions, and sharp sense of humor
- Liam – for your laugh, your goodness, and being my sports buddy
- Lola – for the love notes and art that brighten my day
- Mom and Dad – for your belief in my potential, even when that potential was hidden
- Meg, Sarah, and Garrett – for the irreplaceable bonds of family
- Nana – for your plainspokenness, constant love, and enthusiasm for potato chips
- Karl and Hege – for promoting my work and always being there
- Jeff, Tim, and Josh – for decades of support and friendship
- Eric Clarke – for being a model of humility and leadership
- Brian McLaughlin – for your good nature and steady guidance
- Mike Zaccardi – for believing in this project from the start
- Dr. Naomi Win – for helping me view my work with fresh eyes
- Courtney McQuade – for being a model of soulful wellness

- Tra Williams – for always making time and showing me what's possible
- Stacy Havener – for podcasting excellence and business inspiration
- Neil, Eben, and Max – for showing my family what a perfect day looks like
- Mike and Dallas - for the B.O.I.
- Rusty Vanneman – for impeccable taste in music shared free
- The Resolme and Castro families and the Lake Miramar Ward – *para sa iyong pagkakaibigan at pagmamahal*

To anyone who has ever read one of my books, attended one of my talks, or listened to an episode of Standard Deviations, you have my heartfelt thanks for allowing me to do this work that I love so much.